BRAIN
FOOD

BRAIN
FOOD

Gemma Reece

Introduction by Judith Wills

Love Food® is an imprint of Parragon Books Ltd

Parragon
Queen Street House
4 Queen Street
Bath BA1 1HE

Love Food® and the accompanying heart device is a trade mark of
Parragon Books Ltd

ISBN: 978-1-4075-1746-9
Printed in Indonesia

Produced by the Bridgewater Book Company Ltd
Photographer: Clive Bozzard-Hill
Home economist: Sandra Baddeley

NOTES FOR THE READER
This book uses both metric and imperial measurements. Follow the same units of
measurement throughout; do not mix metric and imperial. All spoon measurements
are level: teaspoons are assumed to be 5 ml, and tablespoons are assumed to be
15 ml. Unless otherwise stated, milk is assumed to be full fat, eggs and individual
vegetables such as potatoes are medium and pepper is freshly ground black pepper.
Recipes using raw or very lightly cooked eggs should be avoided by infants, the
elderly, pregnant women, convalescents and anyone suffering from an illness. The
times given are an approximate guide only.

PICTURE ACKNOWLEDGEMENTS
The publisher would like to thank the following for permission to reproduce
copyright material: Corbis 7; Getty Images 14, 15, 16; iStock 9tl, 9br. Background cover
image and middle image on front cover by Corbis.

Judith Wills is one of the UK's leading diet and nutrition
experts. She is author of *The Food Bible*, *The Diet Bible* and
The Children's Food Bible, and co-author of *Feeding Kids*.
Her website is www.thedietdectective.net

Contents

Introduction   **6**
Can you really eat for a better brain?   6
Fats to feed your brain   8
Other good brain nutrients   10
Brain foods for life   12
Brain food for children   14
Eating plans   16

Soups, Salads and Snacks   **18**
Tomato, Lentil and Red Pepper Soup   21
Ribollito (Tuscan Bean Soup)   21
Gado Gado (Indonesian Warm Salad)   22
Chunky Sweet Potato
   and Butter Bean Soup   24
Italian Fish Soup with White Wine   25
Tuna, Lentil and Potato Salad   27
Rice, Salmon and Pesto Salad   28
Couscous, Nut and Chickpea Pilaf   28
Easy Bean Dip with Crudités   30
Creamy Salmon Baked Potatoes   30
Eggs and Peppers on Toast   33
Quick Smoked Mackerel Pâté   33

Main Courses – Fish and Seafood   **34**
Thai Swordfish Kebabs   37
Swordfish Steaks with Lemon Dressing   37
Spiced Mackerel with Tomato Salad   39
Tuna Steaks with Catalan Sauce   39
Grilled Salmon with Green Lentils
   and Caper Sauce   40
Angler's Filo Pie   42
Salmon Potato Patties with Jalapeño   43
Red Mullet Parcels with Olives   44
Baked Sea Bass with
   White Bean Purée   44
Seafood Provençale   47
Chinese Herring Fillets   47
Seafood Paella with Saffron Rice   48
Chilli Crab Cakes with Stir-fried Greens   50
Teriyaki Prawns with Cashew Nuts   51

Main Courses – Vegetarian and Meat   **52**
Warmly Spiced Vegetable Casserole   54
Ratatouille with Poached Eggs   54
Traditional Spanish Omelette with Herb Salad   56
Red Pepper Felafel with Hummus Dressing   58
Sweet Chilli Chicken with Creole Rice   59
Tray-baked Lamb Steaks with Tomatoes   61
Spicy Chicken with Tortilla Wrap   61
Lamb Kebabs with Greek Salad   62
Turkish Lamb Casserole   62
Chilli Beef with Avocado Salsa   64
Hoisin Beef with Mushrooms   66
Beef Satay with Peanut Sauce   66

Children's Food   **68**
Creamy Salmon Pasta   70
Real Fish Nuggets   71
Tuna Pasta Bake   72
Salmon Fish Cakes   75
Vegetable Fritters   75
Veggie Burgers   76
Cheesy Pasta Bake   76
Thin-crust Vegetable Pizza   79
Butternut and Bean Casserole   80
Three-colour Italian Omelette (Frittata)   81
Meatballs with Tomato Sauce   83
Beef Chow Mein with Beansprouts   83

Breakfasts, Bakes and Desserts   **84**
Yogurt and Strawberry Smoothie   86
Oat and Nut Crunch Mix   86
Fruit Crudités with Chocolate Sauce   89
Fresh Fruit Salad with Blueberries   89
Walnut and Banana Cake   90
Carrot Cake   91
Blueberry and Banana Muffins   92
Oaty Apple and Cinnamon Muffins   92
Chocolate Nut Brownies   95
Walnut and Seed Bread   95
Index   96

Introduction

Can you really eat for a better brain?

The human brain is a powerful organ, but to work well it needs to be provided with good-quality fuel – a balanced diet containing a variety of important nutrients.

How does your brain work?

Your brain is the hub or powerhouse of the central nervous system. It is made up of about a 100 billion nerve cells, and each cell is connected to around 10,000 others. So the total number of connections (neurons) in your brain is approximately 1,000 trillion!

This remarkable control centre enables you to think and make decisions. It also controls your body movements and processes, including speech, sight, hearing and all the other senses. Ideas, planning and emotions begin in the brain, and it is the source of memory and the ability to reason, communicate and solve problems.

How does the right diet influence brainpower and functioning?

Your diet affects the brain chemicals that influence your mood, behaviour, thought processes, learning ability and reactions. Over the past 30 years or so – and especially in the past decade – scientists have been discovering more and more information about how what we eat affects the way our brain functions. We now know that a balanced diet – particularly one that is rich in certain important nutrients such as unsaturated fats, specific amino acids and a variety of vitamins and other micronutrients – really does make a vital contribution to how well our brain works. And on the other hand, if we have a poor diet and lifestyle, brainpower may suffer as a result, both in the short and long term.

What nutrients does the brain need?

Because the brain is so complicated and has so much non-stop work to do, it is no wonder that it needs regular and adequate fuel. Its source of fuel is energy and nutrients from what you eat and drink – and five-star fuel will help it to work at optimum power, and with speed and fluidity.

- The brain's main source of fuel for energy is glucose. This arrives in the brain via the blood, which also supplies it with vital oxygen. The brain requires eight to ten times more glucose and oxygen than the body's other organs, as well as using 20 per cent of the body's oxygen supply, even though it is only around 2 per cent of our total weight. It needs this glucose and oxygen constantly, even as we sleep.

- Because around 60 per cent of the solid matter of your brain is fat (and the working surfaces of your brain neurons are composed of thin layers of fat), you need fat in your diet. The types, amounts and balance of fats that you eat can have a considerable effect on brainpower and health.

- Around 30 per cent of solid brain matter is protein, made up of various amino acids that are mostly used to make and maintain the neurotransmitters (the neuron connectors), which they do with the help of certain vitamins and minerals, which are also of prime importance in the diet. The brain is approximately 77 per cent water, and adequate fluid in the diet is also vital – 1.5–2 litres ($2^3/_4$–$3^1/_2$ pints) a day.

Fats to feed your brain

It is true what our grandmothers used to say: fish really is good for the brain. The special omega-3 fatty acids DHA (docosahexaenoic acid) and EPA (eicosapentaenoic acid) that fish – particularly oily fish – contain (and which form a high percentage of the brain matter itself) are vital for brainpower. Researchers at Washington University in the USA believe that early modern humans had a high omega-3 diet of up to 50 per cent fish and seafood, and that this is what enabled them to learn and evolve at such a fast rate.

Even today, these omega-3 fats (part of the polyunsaturated family of fats) are vital for brain health. They help development in the foetus and in childhood, and can help minimise or prevent brain diseases and problems in later life, such as poor memory or even Alzheimer's disease. Optimum intake of these fats can also, many research studies now seem to show, increase concentration, learning ability and memory, as well as improve negative behaviour.

The 'parent' of the omega-3 group of fats is alpha-linolenic acid (ALA), one of the two 'essential' fats in the diet. ALA is

Leafy greens

ABOVE AND RIGHT A variety of foods contain the types of fat which are good for the brain. While oily fish is one of the best sources of omega-3s, they can also be found in a variety of polyunsaturated nut and seed oils and in leafy greens and some shellfish. Avocados are a good source of mono-unsaturated oils, which are also healthy.

Best sources of omega-3 fats

Food per 100 g/3½ oz	Amount of EPA (mg)	DHA (mg)
FISH		
Halibut	526	393
Herring/sardines, fresh	510	690
Mackerel	710	1100
Sardines, canned in oil	890	820
Salmon, fresh, farmed	618	1293
Sea bass	161	434
Swordfish	108	531
Trout	230	830
Tuna, fresh	283	890
SHELLFISH		
Crabmeat	470	450
Mussels	410	160

Food per 100 g/3½ oz	Amount of omega-3 ALA (g)
OIL	
Flaxseed oil	53
Hemp seed oil	19
Flaxseeds	14
Walnut oil	11.5
Rapeseed oil	9.6
Soya oil	7.3
Pumpkin seeds	7
Walnuts	5.6
Dark leafy greens	1–2

Crabs

Avocado

Pumpkin seeds

Various oils

Oily fish

called essential because our bodies cannot manufacture it, so it has to be provided in what we eat and drink. The body can convert ALA into DHA and EPA (although this conversion is not always super-efficient) and so people who eat little or no fish, such as vegetarians, should ensure that their diets contain plenty of ALA (see box on page 8). Even people who do eat fish will benefit from the extra omega-3s that these foods provide.

How much omega-3 do we need? The UK Food Standards Agency recommends that we all eat at least two portions of fish every week, one of which should be oily, which is equivalent to an average of 450 mg omega-3 (EPA/DHA). Total omega-3 intake (from all sources including plants) should be around 2 g (2,000 mg) a day, according to official European guidelines.

The other branch of the polyunsaturated fats family is the omega-6s. The parent of this family is called linoleic acid and it is another essential fat. But because it is present in large amounts in many of the fats and oils that we choose today – such as corn oil, sunflower oil, safflower oil and blended vegetable oils – many of us eat too much of this type of oil. It seems that a ratio between 5:1 and 2:1 may be ideal, whereas in the West, the ratio could be as high as 18:1. Experts now believe that it is the correct balance of omega-6s to omega-3s in the diet that can help us achieve and maintain good health.

A high intake of omega-6 fats – and saturated and trans fats – can block the good work of the omega-3s, so the ideal diet is one that supplies smaller amounts of omega-6s and higher amounts of omega-3s than we presently consume.

One good way of reducing the amount of omega-6s that we eat is to consume more monounsaturated fats (found in olive oil, rapeseed oil, groundnut oil, walnut oil or avocado) rather than highly polyunsaturated oils.

Other good brain nutrients

It is not just omega-3 fatty acids that can help feed the brain – a range of other nutrients have a significant role to play in helping brainpower and memory and protecting the brain from degeneration.

Antioxidants

Brain cells are especially vulnerable to attack by free radicals – molecular by-products of normal living that can be harmful in excess. These are 'mopped up' and their production inhibited in the body by various compounds in the diet, which have been named 'antioxidants'. A high-antioxidant diet can significantly reduce the risk of cognitive loss – memory, judgement and reasoning – and vitamin C can increase blood flow to the brain.

Some vitamins (such as C and E) and minerals (such as zinc and selenium) are powerful antioxidants, while many vegetables, fruits and other plant foods contain antioxidant compounds, most of which have been analysed and named only in recent years. Some of the plant chemicals with the strongest link to a healthy brain are the carotenoid group and the flavonoid group.

Choline

A vitamin-like component of the fatty acid lecithin, choline is used in our bodies to maintain cell membranes and transmit nerve impulses, and it is essential for optimum brain development in the young. It has also been claimed that choline may help prevent memory loss and improve cognitive function in older people. Traces of choline are found in many foods, but eggs are a particularly rich source of choline. Other sources include soybeans, cooked beef, chicken livers and spinach.

L-tyrosine

L-tyrosine is an amino acid – a building block of protein. All the 22 amino acids are used to make the neurotransmitters (the neuron connectors) that allow your brain cells to communicate, but l-tyrosine is especially important for increasing alertness. As the brain consists of 8 per cent protein as a whole, a diet reasonably high in protein is important. Foods such as lean meat, eggs, cheese, fish, poultry and pulses are good high-protein foods.

Nutrient	Best sources	How much you need
ANTIOXIDANTS		
Vitamin C	Berry fruits, citrus fruits, kiwi fruit, peppers and green vegetables.	UK 40 mg/EC 60 mg/USA 75 mg.* Cannot be stored in the body, so needed daily.
Vitamin E	Olive oil, avocados, nuts, seeds and plant oils.	UK 5 mg/EC 10 mg/USA 15 mg.
Carotenoids	Carrots, red peppers, tomatoes, squashes, sweet potatoes, mangoes and dark leafy greens.	No official RDAs for total carotenoids, but aim for 1–2 portions of orange or red plant food a day.
Flavonoids	Red and purple berries, currants and grapes, olives, citrus fruits, onions, apples, leeks, garlic, fresh peas and beans, leafy greens, fresh herbs and spices.	No official RDAs for flavonoids, but aim for 1 portion of flavonoid-rich food at every meal.
Choline	Eggs, wheatgerm, cabbage, peanuts, soya beans, sardines**, wholegrains, peas and beef.	No official RDAs for choline, but aim for 1–2 portions of choline-rich food a day.
L-tyrosine	Mature hard cheese, milk, meat, oats, wholegrains, avocados, almonds and turkey.	No official RDAs for this specific amino acid, but total average requirement for adult male UK 45 g/USA 56 g; adult female UK 36 g/USA 46 g.

* In general, USA and EC recommended daily amounts (RDAs for vitamins and minerals are higher than those in the UK. ** For fish and sources of omega-3s, see page 8)

Nutrient	Best sources	How much you need
B VITAMINS		
Vitamin B1 (thiamine)	Wholegrain and enriched-grain products such as fortified cereals, rice, pasta and bread.	UK 0.8 mg (f); 1 mg (m)/EC 1.4 mg/USA 1.1 mg (f); 1.2 mg (m).
Vitamin B6 (pyridoxine)	Found in chicken, fish, pork, liver, wholegrain cereals and nuts.	UK 1.2 mg (f); 1.4 mg (m)/EC 2 mg/USA 1.3 mg.
Folate (folic acid)	Found in fortified cereals, bananas, oranges, lemons, strawberries, leafy vegetables and pulses.	UK 200 ug/EC 200 ug/USA 400 ug.
Vitamin B12 (cyanocobalamin)	Found in eggs, milk and dairy products, meat, fish and poultry.	UK 1.5 ug/EC 1 ug/USA 2.4 ug.
MINERALS		
Selenium	Seafood, Brazil nuts, lentils, wholewheat and pork.	UK 60 ug/EC no RDA/USA 55 ug.
Magnesium	Nuts, wholegrains, fresh peas and beans, green vegetables and cocoa powder.	UK 270 mg/ EC 300 mg/USA 320 mg (f); 420 mg (m).
Zinc	Shellfish, nuts and seeds, wholegrains, lean red meat and mature hard cheese.	UK 7 mg (f); 9.5 mg (m)/EC 15 mg/USA 8 mg (f); 11 mg (m).
Iron	Red meat, pulses, leafy greens, wholegrains, seeds, dried fruit and eggs.	UK 14.8 mg (f); 8.7 mg (m)/EC 14 mg/USA 18 mg (f); 8 mg (m).
Low-GI foods	Pulses, oats, rye, pasta, fruit, wholegrain breads, yogurt and green vegetables.	Aim to choose low-GI foods at every meal.

B vitamins

The vitamin B group is vital for brain function.

Vitamin B1 (thiamine) helps to release energy from carbohydrates for a healthy brain and nerve cells. It is found in wholegrain and enriched-grain products.

Vitamin B6 (pyridoxine) is vital for the metabolism of l-tyrosine and the other amino acids.

Folate (folic acid) is vital for fatty acid and amino acid metabolism in the brain and prevention of neural tube defects in unborn babies.

Vitamin B12 (cyanocobalamin) is vital for healthy nervous tissue, converting carbohydrates into brain energy, metabolizing essential fats for the brain and helping build and maintain healthy nerve cells.

Minerals

Important minerals include: selenium, which helps the work of vitamin E; magnesium, an aid to the smooth running of the brain; and iron, vital for transporting oxygen to the brain.

Other factors

Regular eating is important to provide the constant glucose supply that your brain needs. A diet containing plenty of low-glycaemic index (GI) foods will help, as these are less quickly absorbed by the bloodstream and help to keep blood sugar levels constant. Breakfast is a vital meal of the day for brain functioning after the long night's fast.

What not to eat

Some foods can have a negative effect on the brain. A diet high in saturated and trans fats (such as full-fat dairy produce, fatty cuts of meat, pastry, biscuits, cakes, processed desserts and crisps) can block the work of the 'good' omega-3 fatty acids, and so it is important to try to cut right back on these in your diet. A high intake of alcohol is also linked with brain degeneration, and a typical 'junk food' diet will probably not contain all the nutrients your brain needs for good health.

Brain foods for life

Throughout your life, what you eat can help your brain to function well. The following offers an insight into how brain foods can affect different life stages.

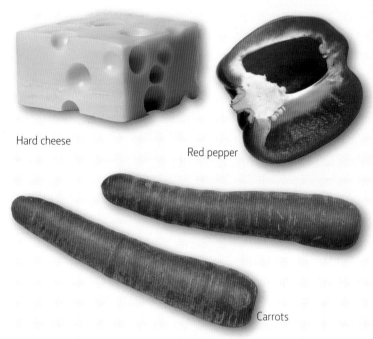

Hard cheese

Red pepper

Carrots

Before birth, and infancy

While a baby is in the womb, his or her brain grows more rapidly than in any other stage of infant or child development, and faster than any other part of the body. During the first year after birth, the brain continues to grow rapidly, tripling in size by an infant's first birthday.

● Neural tube defects (NTDs) of the spinal chord and brain are one of the most common birth defects and can be prevented by adequate folate (folic acid) in the mother's diet.

● A high alcohol consumption during pregnancy can increase the risk of hyperactivity, attention deficiency and emotional problems in children.

● Research on a large group of pregnant women, published in *The Lancet* in 2007, has found that low omega-3 diets during pregnancy can result in children with suboptimal brain development and with reduced verbal IQ.

● Some researchers have also found that low omega-3 diets during pregnancy can result in children who experience increased behaviour problems.

● Research on animals published in the *New Scientist* in 2004 found that extra choline in the diet while a woman is pregnant may improve her child's brainpower.

● Infants who have low amounts of DHA in their diet have reduced brain development and diminished visual clarity.

● The increased intelligence and academic performance of breastfed compared with formula-fed infants may be attributed in part to the higher DHA content of human milk.

Childhood

A variety of scientific trials show that children who eat an optimum range of nutrients have improved IQ, concentration and memory.

● Research on schoolchildren in Durham in north-east England has shown that a regular intake of omega-3 oils can have a significant impact upon learning, attention, memory, reading ability and behaviour. Some children improved by as much as four academic years in a six-month trial. While the research is carried out using supplements, it is reasonable to assume that a diet high in foods naturally rich in omega-3s would have a similar effect.

● A balanced, nutrient-rich breakfast is a vital meal of the day for kids. Several research trials have found that those who have only high-sugar, high-GI drinks or foods at breakfast – or no breakfast at all – perform significantly less well at tasks requiring concentration, memory and alertness.

● The right diet plays an important role in helping older children and teenagers both to revise for and to perform more effectively during exams.

Tomatoes

Eggs

Oranges

LEFT Hard cheese is an excellent source of l-tyrosine which can help improve alertness and memory as we age. Red peppers and carrots are both excellent sources of antioxidant carotenoids, while peppers are also rich in vitamin C, another antioxidant. These can help improve cognitive power.

ABOVE Tomatoes are rich in both carotenoids and vitamin C – the deeper the colours, the more carotene they contain. Eggs are one of the best sources of choline, which is essential for brain development in the young. Oranges are high in vitamin C and flavonoids, which help blood flow to the brain and mop up 'free radicals' that can harm the brain.

• The long-chain omega-6 fatty acid GLA (gamma-linoleic acid), found in evening primrose and starflower oils, may also help children's brain function.

• Fish oil and evening primrose oil can also help to combat the problems of dyslexia and ADHD (attention deficit hyperactivity disorder).

Adulthood

As we get older and face the normal stresses and problems of everyday life, a balanced diet containing adequate omega-3 and other 'brain foods' can help us to maintain brainpower. It can also help avoid problems that could affect us later in life such as loss of memory, Alzheimer's disease and depression.

• L-tyrosine becomes depleted when we are under stress and supplementing with tyrosine-rich foods (see page 10) may improve alertness and memory.

• In a UK survey of 14,500 families, pregnant women with diets low in omega-6s were found to have an increased risk of suffering from depression.

Old age

Even into old age, brain foods can help keep us alert and ward off fading memory and other typical problems such as lack of concentration and mental stamina.

• In a study published in *Psychosomatic Medicine* in 2007 in the USA, older adults who had diets high in omega-6 fatty acids and low in omega-3 fatty acids appeared to be more prone to depression and stress.

• According to research carried out in 2006 by the Department of Psychological and Brain Sciences, Duke University, North Carolina, USA, low levels of choline are associated with Alzheimer's disease, and boosting dietary intake (see page 10) may slow memory loss in old age.

• Research carried out on ageing dogs has shown that a high intake of antioxidant-rich foods can improve cognitive skills.

• It is vital to keep a healthy blood flow to the brain as we age and a diet rich in omega-3s and antioxidants, plus regular exercise, is probably a major key to healthy circulation and continuing brain health.

Brain food for children

Knowing what to feed your children for good brain health is one thing, but getting them to eat it is quite another. However, changes can be successfully achieved by following these simple tips.

• Children's diet begins with what you buy at the supermarket. Don't be swayed in your choices.

• Encourage your children to be interested in what they eat and why good food is important for them. Most small children love helping with food in the kitchen and most will try items such as vegetables if they have helped to shop for or prepare them.

• Sometimes fussy and poor eaters eat better when the portions are small – they can be discouraged when faced with a large plateful. Over time you can increase the amounts. Toddlers and small children often eat better when offered finger foods.

• Only serve one new food at a time, offer a very small amount and serve a new food with a familiar food.

• Let children develop a good natural appetite for their meals by avoiding giving them large between-meal snacks or high-calorie drinks. Do not give them any snacks in the hour before mealtime.

Tips for increasing brain food intake
Vegetables
• If you have a garden, let your children cultivate some quick-growing lettuce and radish – growing their own will encourage them to eat salad items.

• Prepare vegetables in a cheese sauce and/or with pasta and/or in an oven bake.

• Blend vegetables into smooth soups or add very small chunks to a meat or chicken casserole.

• Overcooked and soggy vegetables are a discouragement for most children – stir-frying or baking are more appealing ways to cook them.

• Children often enjoy crunching on crisp, raw fresh vegetables cut into strips to be eaten with fingers – with a tasty dip, perhaps.

• Serve a very finely chopped or puréed vegetable sauce with pasta, rice or a baked potato.

Fish
• Almost all children love fish nuggets, cakes or fingers, and they are all very easy – and healthier – to make at home (see Real Fish Nuggets on page 71).

• Most children love a potato-topped cheesy fish pie. Try a sweet potato topping for a healthier option. Fish kebabs threaded with cherry tomatoes are another good idea.

• To encourage children to eat more oily fish, try salmon fish fingers or make a pasta dish with salmon or fresh tuna flakes. Salmon or mackerel pâté is easy to make and an ideal sandwich filler.

Swap to brain food

● Swap a bag of crisps for a small handful of almonds, Brazil nuts or cashew nuts (for children aged over five years).

● Swap a pack of sweets or a chocolate bar for a small bag you have made up yourself containing a few chocolate chips, a few pieces of dried fruit and a few nuts.

● Swap a slice of white bread and jam for a rice cake topped with a little nut butter (butter blended with ground nuts).

● Swap a slice of sponge cake for one of the brain-friendly bakes in the section on Breakfast, Bakes and Desserts.

Lunch boxes

An ideal packed lunch will contain a good balance of nutrients – some protein, good-quality carbohydrate, some fat and a good range of vitamins and minerals, always including some vitamin C. The ideal drink is water – occasionally milk or diluted fruit juice are fine, but whole fruit is better than juice, as it provides more nutrients, is better for blood sugars and is less likely to contribute to tooth decay.

Five complete lunch-box meals

The following meals are for children aged 5 years or more:

1 Sandwich of granary bread filled with tuna mashed with natural yogurt and lemon juice; 3 cherry tomatoes; 1 small apple; 1 slice of Carrot Cake.

2 1 wholemeal pitta bread filled with hummus and a selection of chopped vegetables; 1 individual pot of natural bio yogurt with honey; 1 Oaty Apple and Cinnamon Muffin; 1 satsuma.

3 1 box of home-made pasta salad with chicken or Cheddar cheese, chopped red pepper, cucumber, red onion, pumpkin seeds and olive oil and lemon dressing; 1 slice of rich fruit cake; 1 plum.

4 Wholemeal roll filled with hard-boiled egg, tomato and watercress; handful of red grapes; 1 slice of Walnut and Banana Cake; 1 individual pot of low-fat fromage frais.

Brain food recipes

This book contains a section of recipes specifically aimed at children, but most of the recipes in the other sections are also highly suitable for children – the symbol © means 'suitable for children' and, if necessary, a minimum age is given in addition. Always check that your child is older than the minimum age stated if serving the dish to them.

Other recipes in this book that are likely to appeal to most children are:

● Tomato, Lentil and Red Pepper Soup
● Creamy Salmon Baked Potatoes
● Tuna Steaks with Catalan Sauce
● Angler's Filo Pie
● Salmon Potato Patties with Jalapeño (use mild chillies)
● Teriyaki Prawns with Cashew Nuts
● Traditional Spanish Omelette with Herb Salad
● Ratatouille with Poached Eggs (only for children aged over 5 because of the lightly cooked egg)
● Sweet Chilli Chicken with Creole Rice
● Lamb Kebabs with Greek Salad
● Spicy Chicken with Tortilla Wrap
● Hoisin Beef with Mushrooms
● Any of the recipes in the Breakfasts, Bakes and Desserts section.

5 Sandwich of wholemeal bread filled with salmon mashed with natural fromage frais, cucumber and spring onion slices; carrot batons; 1 small pack of dried mixed fruit or sultanas. Add a drink of water to every box for vital hydration.

Eating plans

A balanced and nutritious diet for the brain isn't simply about individual nutrients or foods – you need a variety of foods each day to ensure that you really do eat to improve brainpower.

Each plan contains a selection of recipes from this book, as well as several non-recipe meals. Each day's eating not only provides high levels of the important 'brain foods' mentioned in this chapter, but also gives a balanced and healthy diet overall, high in fruits and vegetables and reasonably low in sodium and low in so-called 'junk' foods. Don't forget to drink adequate fluid. Aim for approximately 1.5–2 litres (2³/₄–3¹/₂ pints) a day – water is ideal.

Children's Eating Plan

BREAKFAST	LUNCH	SUPPER
Monday		
Porridge made with semi-skimmed milk and a handful of mixed dried fruit added. 1 satsuma	Packed lunch (see page 15) or low-salt, low-sugar baked beans on wholemeal toast topped with 1 tablespoon grated mature Cheddar cheese. 1 apple	Salmon Fish Cake with peas and grilled tomato. 1 individual pot of low-fat fruit yogurt
Tuesday		
1 slice of wholemeal toast with smooth peanut butter (aged over 1 year). 1 individual pot of low-fat fruit fromage frais. 1 plum	Packed lunch (see page 15) or poached egg (soft-poached only for children aged 3 years or more) on wholemeal toast. 1 orange	Butternut and Bean Casserole. Broccoli
Wednesday		
Wheat-based biscuit cereal with semi-skimmed milk and a handful of fresh berries. 1 slice of wholemeal toast with yeast extract savoury spread	Packed lunch (see page 15) or cooked chicken breast slices tossed with chopped raw vegetables and cooked brown rice	Thin-crust Vegetable Pizza. Mixed-leaf side salad. 1 pear or nectarine
Thursday		
Low-fat Greek-style yogurt topped with Fresh Fruit Salad with Blueberries and a handful of any wholegrain cereal	Packed lunch (see page 15) or Tomato, Lentil and Red Pepper Soup. 1 wholemeal roll. 1 individual pot of low-fat fromage frais	Tuna Pasta Bake. Mixed-leaf side salad. 1 apple
Friday		
As Monday	Packed lunch (see page 15) or hummus, wholemeal pitta bread and chopped salad. 1 individual pot of low-fat fruit yogurt	Meatballs with Tomato Sauce. Brown rice. Mangetout

BREAKFAST	LUNCH	SUPPER
Saturday		
Yogurt and Strawberry Smoothie. 2 oatcakes	Creamy Salmon Baked Potato. Baked tomatoes.	Veggie Burger served with oven chips and peas or low-salt, low-sugar baked beans. 1 satsuma
Sunday		
1–2 boiled eggs. 1–2 slices of wholemeal bread. 1 orange	Lean roast beef, new potatoes, dark green cabbage, carrots, peas. Fresh Fruit Salad with Blueberries topped with Oat and Nut Crunch Mix and natural fromage frais	Chunky Sweet Potato and Butter Bean Soup. 1 individual pot of low-fat fruit yogurt

Adults' Eating Plan

Monday		
Muesli topped with blueberries and skimmed milk	Avocado and walnut salad with dark salad leaves and olive oil dressing. 1 slice of Walnut and Seed Bread. 1 apple	Tray-baked Lamb Steaks with Tomatoes. Steamed broccoli
Tuesday		
Porridge made with water and skimmed milk sprinkled with pumpkin seeds. $\frac{1}{2}$ pink grapefruit	Quick Smoked Mackerel Pâté. 2–3 Oatcakes. Watercress and cherry tomatoes	Sweet Chilli Chicken with Creole Rice. Mixed-leaf side salad. Fresh Fruit Salad with Blueberries
Wednesday		
1 Oaty Apple and Cinnamon Muffin. 1 individual pot of low-fat natural bio yogurt. 1 orange	Couscous, Nut and Chickpea Pilaf. Handful of red grapes.	Baked Sea Bass with White Bean Purée. Steamed green beans and mangetout.
Thursday		
Yogurt and Strawberry Smoothie	Tuna, Lentil and Potato Salad. Handful of red grapes	Red Pepper Felafel with Hummus Dressing. Wholewheat pasta shapes. Rocket and spinach salad
Friday		
As Monday	Spicy Chicken with Tortilla Wrap. 1 apple	Traditional Spanish Omelette with Herb Salad. 1 orange
Saturday		
1 individual pot of low-fat natural bio yogurt topped with Fresh Fruit Salad with Blueberries and a handful of Oat and Nut Crunch Mix	Ribollito (Tuscan Bean Soup)	Hoisin Beef with Mushrooms. Brown basmati rice
Sunday		
1–2 boiled eggs. 1–2 slices of wholegrain bread. 1 orange	Lean roast pork, dark green cabbage or kale, carrots, sweet potato and peas. Fruit Crudités with Chocolate Sauce	30–40-g (1–1½-oz) portion of mature Cheddar cheese. 2–3 oatcakes. Tomato and celery sticks

NB: Portion sizes in the above Eating Plans should be tailored to individual needs; amounts given are guides only

Soups, Salads and Snacks

Within this chapter you will find plenty of healthy ideas for quick and easy lunches and suppers, whatever the time of year. Soups are ideal for getting plenty of vegetables and pulses into your diet, while salads and snacks can be a great way to eat carbohydrates, protein, vegetables, nuts and seeds.

KEY

Ⓥ Suitable for vegetarians

Ⓓ Ideal for weight control

Ⓟ Suitable for pregnancy

Ⓒ Suitable for children

Ⓠ Quick to prepare and cook

Ⓛ Low cost

Tomato, Lentil and Red Pepper Soup

NUTRITION NOTES This soup is rich in carotenes, vitamin C and vitamin E, all antioxidants that are vital for the healthy oxygenation of the brain and to protect against free radicals. Lentils are rich in iron to help memory and learning power, and also in selenium, which works with vitamin E to increase the beneficial effects of both.

SERVES 4 Ⓥ Ⓓ Ⓟ Ⓒ Ⓛ

3 tbsp olive oil

2 onions, chopped

2 garlic cloves, chopped

2 large red peppers, deseeded and chopped

500 g/1 lb 2 oz ripe tomatoes, chopped

100 g/3½ oz red split lentils

600 ml/1 pint vegetable stock, plus extra to thin (optional)

1 tbsp red wine vinegar

salt and pepper

2 spring onions, chopped, or 1 tbsp snipped fresh chives, to garnish

1 Heat the oil in a large frying pan over a medium-high heat, add the onions and cook, stirring, for 5 minutes, or until softened but not browned. Add the garlic and red peppers and cook, stirring, for 5 minutes, or until the red peppers are softened.

2 Add the tomatoes, lentils and stock and bring to a simmer. Reduce the heat to low, cover and simmer gently for 25 minutes, or until the lentils are tender. Stir in the vinegar and season with a little salt and pepper to taste.

3 Leave to cool slightly, then transfer the soup to a blender or food processor and blend for 1 minute, or until smooth. Return to the frying pan and reheat, stirring in a little hot water or stock if the soup seems a little too thick.

4 Serve in warmed bowls, garnished with the spring onions.

Cook's Tip

* The soup is also good served cold.

Ribollito (Tuscan Bean Soup)

NUTRITION NOTES This soup is packed with brain-friendly nutrients, including protein, vitamin C, magnesium, choline, carotene, lutein, vitamin E and omega-3 fatty acids.

SERVES 4–6 Ⓥ Ⓓ Ⓟ Ⓒ Ⓛ

2 tbsp olive oil

1 large red onion, sliced

2 celery sticks, chopped

1 large carrot, roughly chopped

2 large garlic cloves, chopped

400 g/14 oz canned chopped tomatoes with herbs

400 g/14 oz canned cannellini or borlotti beans, drained and rinsed

250 g/9 oz cavolo nero (Italian black cabbage), kale or Savoy cabbage

600 ml/1 pint vegetable or chicken stock

75 g/2¾ oz stale white or wholemeal breadcrumbs

2 tbsp chopped fresh flat-leaf parsley

salt and pepper

1 Heat the oil in a large saucepan over a medium heat, add the onion, celery, carrot and garlic and cook, stirring frequently, for 8–10 minutes, or until softened.

2 Add the tomatoes and their juice, beans, cavolo nero and stock, stir well and bring to a simmer. Crush some of the beans against the side of the saucepan to help thicken the soup. Cover and cook over a low heat for 45 minutes–1 hour, or until all the vegetables are tender. Season with a little salt and pepper to taste. If you have time, leave the soup to stand for a few hours to thicken up and for the flavours to develop.

3 Sprinkle the breadcrumbs and parsley over the soup 30 minutes before you are ready to serve and reheat, uncovered, over a low heat (or see Cook's Tip). The soup should be quite thick, with not much liquid remaining.

4 Spoon into warmed bowls to serve.

Cook's Tip

* You can cook the soup in a flameproof casserole, then, for Step 3, transfer to a preheated oven at 190°C/375°F/Gas Mark 5 and cook, uncovered, for 30 minutes to brown the breadcrumbs lightly.

Gado Gado (Indonesian Warm Salad)

NUTRITION NOTES This salad is a great source of choline, carotene, iron and vitamins C and E.

SERVES 4 Ⓥ Ⓟ Ⓒ (aged over 1 year), Ⓛ
8 outer leaves of cos lettuce or similar dark, crisp lettuce leaves
100 g/3¹/₂ oz green beans, lightly cooked
100 g/3¹/₂ oz baby carrots, lightly cooked
250 g/9 oz salad new potatoes, such as Charlotte, cooked until just tender
1 tbsp groundnut oil
125 g/4¹/₂ oz fresh beansprouts
8-cm/3¹/₄-inch piece cucumber, deseeded and cut into 4-cm/1¹/₂-inch batons
4 eggs, hard-boiled
1 small mild onion, sliced into rings

SAUCE
4 tbsp canned reduced-fat coconut milk
3 tbsp sugar-free smooth peanut butter
juice of ¹/₂ lime
2 tsp light soy sauce
dash of Tabasco sauce or any chilli sauce

1 Roughly tear the lettuce leaves, if large, and arrange on 4 individual serving plates or 1 large serving platter. Halve the beans and cut the carrots, as necessary, into batons. Arrange these with the potatoes (cut into chunks if large) on the plates or platter.

2 Heat the oil in a non-stick frying pan or wok over a high heat, add the beansprouts and stir-fry for 2 minutes until lightly cooked but still crisp. Remove with a slotted spoon and sprinkle over the cooked vegetables with the cucumber. Peel and quarter the eggs, then arrange on top of the salad.

3 Add the onion rings to the oil remaining in the frying pan or wok and stir-fry over a high heat for 5 minutes, or until golden and crisp. Combine all the ingredients for the sauce in a small bowl and pour over the salad. Top with the onion rings and serve immediately.

Cook's Tips
* This dish is best served when all the cooked vegetables are still warm. It is a superb special-occasion main course salad for vegetarians.
* To save time, you could buy ready-made peanut (satay) sauce and thin it with a little canned reduced-fat coconut milk.
* For diners over 5 years old, you can sprinkle chopped peanuts and/or sesame seeds over the top to garnish.

Chunky Sweet Potato and Butter Bean Soup

NUTRITION NOTES Orange-fleshed sweet potatoes are a brilliant source of vitamins A, C and E – powerful antioxidants – while pulses are a good source of choline and folate.

SERVES 4 ⓥ ⓓ ⓟ ⓒ ⓠ ⓛ

2 tbsp olive oil

1 onion, chopped

2 celery sticks, chopped

1 large carrot, roughly chopped

1 large or 2 small sweet potatoes, peeled and chopped

400 g/14 oz canned butter beans or cannellini beans, drained and rinsed

1 litre/1³/₄ pints vegetable stock

1 large handful fresh coriander leaves

2 tbsp freshly grated Parmesan cheese

salt and pepper

1 Heat the oil in a large saucepan over a medium heat, add the onion, celery and carrot and cook, stirring frequently, for 8–10 minutes, or until softened. Add the sweet potatoes and beans and cook, stirring, for 1 minute.

2 Add the stock, stir thoroughly and bring to a simmer. Season with a little salt and pepper to taste. Cover, reduce the heat and cook for 25–30 minutes until all the vegetables are tender.

3 Leave to cool slightly, then transfer one-third of the soup to a blender or food processor and blend until smooth. Return to the saucepan and mix in well. Check the seasoning and reheat.

4 Ladle into warmed bowls and scatter with the coriander and Parmesan cheese before serving.

Variations

* You can blend all the soup for a change, to make a smooth vegetable soup.
* You can use dried pulses in any recipe that features canned beans – follow the pack instructions for preparing and cooking; many require presoaking overnight and lengthy cooking times.

Italian Fish Soup with White Wine

NUTRITION NOTES This fish soup is a good source of omega-3 fatty acids, selenium and zinc, and contains vegetables rich in antioxidants for a healthy brain.

SERVES 4 Ⓓ Ⓟ Ⓒ (aged over 5 years), Ⓠ
4 tbsp olive oil
3 leeks, sliced
2 celery sticks, chopped
1 large onion, chopped
2 large garlic cloves, well crushed
250 g/9 oz chestnut mushrooms, sliced
1 litre/1³/₄ pints fish stock
250 g/9 oz canned tomatoes
100 ml/3¹/₂ fl oz Italian dry white wine
1 tsp hot paprika
450 g/1 lb mixed fish fillets, such as cod, sea bass, monkfish, red
    mullet and sea bream, cut into bite-sized pieces
450 g/1 lb mixed raw seafood, such as prawns in their shells, cleaned
    mussels in their shells, cleaned squid, cut into rings and tentacles
    chopped, and crabmeat (cooked), including claws
salt and pepper
plenty of chopped fresh flat-leaf parsley, to garnish

1 Heat the oil in a large saucepan or flameproof casserole over a medium heat, add the leeks, celery, onion and garlic and cook, stirring frequently, for 8–10 minutes, or until softened. Add the mushrooms, stock, tomatoes and their juice and wine and stir well.

2 Bring to a simmer and add the paprika and a little salt and pepper to taste. Then add all the fish and seafood and simmer gently for 15 minutes. Check the seasoning.

3 Serve in warmed bowls, garnished with the parsley.

Cook's Tips
* Clean mussels by scrubbing or scraping the shells and pulling out any beards attached to the mussels. Discard any opened mussels or mussels with broken shells. Discard closed mussels after cooking.
* Shellfish is one of the foods likely to cause an allergic reaction in children, but non-allergic children can eat this soup, or you could substitute other fish for the shellfish.

Tuna, Lentil and Potato Salad

NUTRITION NOTES This soup is high in omega-3 fatty acids, vitamin B6, folate and vitamin E.

SERVES 4 ℗ © ⓦ

200 g/7 oz Puy or brown lentils

2 tbsp olive oil, plus extra for brushing

300 g/10¹/₂ oz baby new potatoes, washed

1 head Little Gem lettuce

4 fresh tuna steaks, about 100 g/3¹/₂ oz each

12 small cherry tomatoes, halved

40 g/1¹/₂ oz rocket leaves

salt and pepper

DRESSING

5 tbsp fruity olive oil

1 tbsp balsamic vinegar

2 tsp red wine vinegar

1 tsp smooth Dijon mustard

1 tsp soft light brown sugar

1 Cook the lentils in a saucepan of boiling water for 25 minutes, or until tender. Drain, tip into a bowl and stir in the oil.

2 Meanwhile, cook the potatoes in a separate saucepan of lightly salted water for 15 minutes, or until just tender.

3 Break off the outer lettuce leaves and cut the heart into 8 evenly sized pieces. Arrange on 4 individual serving plates.

4 Put all the ingredients for the dressing, with a little salt and pepper to taste, in a screw-top jar and shake well to combine.

5 When the potatoes are nearly cooked, lightly brush a ridged griddle pan with oil and heat over a high heat. When very hot, add the tuna steaks and cook for 1¹/₂ minutes on each side to sear. Remove to a chopping board and cut each steak into 6 chunks.

6 Drain the potatoes and roughly chop any larger ones. Arrange with the lentils, tuna and tomatoes on the serving plates, sprinkle over the rocket leaves and spoon over the dressing. Serve immediately.

Cook's Tips

* If you don't have a griddle pan, you can cook the tuna steaks in a non-stick frying pan lightly brushed with olive oil.

* To save time, you can make a large batch of the dressing in a screw-top jar – it will keep for several weeks in the refrigerator. Leave at room temperature for 1 hour and shake well before using.

Rice, Salmon and Pesto Salad

NUTRITION NOTES This salad is rich in omega-3 fatty acids, vitamin E, magnesium, iron and zinc.

SERVES 4 Ⓟ © (aged over 5 years), Ⓠ Ⓛ
250 g/9 oz brown basmati rice
3 garlic cloves, peeled
1 tsp sea salt
1 large handful fresh basil sprigs
5 tbsp olive oil, plus extra for drizzling
100 g/3¹/₂ oz pine kernels
400 g/14 oz skinless salmon fillets
pepper

1 Cook the rice according to the packet instructions using the absorption method – with standard brown basmati rice, this should take around 30 minutes. Once tender, leave the rice in the saucepan, covered, off the heat.

2 Meanwhile, to make the pesto, put the garlic cloves and salt in a mortar and thoroughly crush with a pestle. Remove the stalks from the basil and add three-quarters of the basil leaves to the mortar with 2 tablespoons of the oil. Crush again, then add half the pine kernels with a further 2 tablespoons of the remaining oil and pepper to taste. Pound again until you have a thick paste.

3 Heat the remaining 1 tablespoon of oil in a large, non-stick frying pan over a high heat. When hot, add the salmon fillets and cook for 1¹/₂ minutes on each side to sear. Reduce the heat and cook for a further 1–2 minutes, or until the fish is done to your liking (don't overcook), adding the remaining pine kernels to the frying pan to cook, stirring, until golden. Remove the salmon and pine kernels from the frying pan. Flake the salmon flesh into large pieces.

4 Lightly combine the rice, salmon flakes and pesto in a salad bowl. Top with the remaining basil leaves, the toasted pine kernels and a drizzle of oil.

Cook's Tip
* You can use white basmati rice if you prefer, but you will lose B vitamins.

Couscous, Nut and Chickpea Pilaf

NUTRITION NOTES This dish is a good source of l-tyrosine, iron, vitamin B6, folate, omega-3 fatty acids, selenium, vitamin E and zinc.

SERVES 4 Ⓥ Ⓓ Ⓟ © (aged over 5 years), Ⓠ Ⓛ
200 g/7 oz quick-cook couscous (see Cook's Tips)
350 ml/12 fl oz vegetable stock
1 large yellow pepper, deseeded and chopped
4 spring onions, chopped
10 ready-to-eat dried apricots, chopped
50 g/1³/₄ oz sultanas
50 g/1³/₄ oz flaked almonds, toasted
50 g/1³/₄ oz walnut pieces
1 heaped tablespoon pumpkin seeds
150 g/5¹/₂ oz drained, canned chickpeas, rinsed
2 tbsp pumpkin seed oil

1 Put the couscous in a large, heatproof bowl. Heat the stock in a saucepan to boiling point, then pour over the couscous and stir well. Cover and leave to stand for 15 minutes, by which time all the liquid should have been absorbed.

2 Stir all the remaining ingredients, except the oil, into the couscous, forking through lightly. Serve drizzled with the oil.

Cook's Tips
* This recipe uses quick-cook couscous, but if you have more time, you can buy traditional couscous (from health-food stores), which contains more iron and B vitamins. Follow the packet instructions to prepare.
* Pumpkin seed oil makes a tasty change from olive oil, is high in omega-3 fatty acids and is now widely available.

Variation
* You can use whatever nuts and seeds you like – try cashew nuts, pine kernels or sunflower seeds.

Easy Bean Dip with Crudités

NUTRITION NOTES This pâté is a good source of vitamins B1, B6, B12, C and E, carotene, iron and zinc.

SERVES 4 Ⓥ Ⓓ Ⓟ Ⓒ (aged over 1 year), Ⓠ Ⓛ
400 g/14 oz canned cannellini beans, drained and rinsed
150 g/5½ oz Greek-style yogurt
1 large garlic clove, well crushed
1 heaped tbsp sun-dried tomato paste
1 bottled or canned red pepper, drained and chopped
selection of crudités, such as carrots, celery, peppers, onion and
    cucumber, cut into batons or strips, and/or lettuce hearts, leaves
    separated, and lightly cooked asparagus tips or baby sweetcorn,
    cooled, about 500 g/1 lb 2 oz in total
salt and pepper

1 Put all the ingredients, except the crudités, in a blender or food processor and blend for 1 minute. Spoon into a bowl, cover and chill in the refrigerator for 30 minutes.

2 Meanwhile, prepare the crudités. Arrange on a platter and serve with the chilled dip.

Cook's Tip
* Use half the yogurt mixture to make a delicious pâté or sandwich filling instead of a dip.

Variations
* You can use butter beans in place of the cannellini beans.

Creamy Salmon Baked Potatoes

NUTRITION NOTES This potato dish is a good source of omega-3 fatty acids and vitamins B6, B12, C and E.

SERVES 4 Ⓓ Ⓟ Ⓒ Ⓠ Ⓛ
4 baking potatoes, about 275 g/9¾ oz each, scrubbed
250 g/9 oz skinless salmon fillet
200 g/7 oz reduced-fat soft cheese
2–3 tbsp skimmed milk
2 tbsp chopped/snipped fresh herbs, such as dill or chives
60 g/2½ oz mature Cheddar cheese, grated
salt and pepper

1 Preheat the oven to 200°C/400°F/Gas Mark 6. Prick the skins of the potatoes and put on the top shelf of the preheated oven. Bake for 50–60 minutes until the skins are crisp and the centres are soft when pierced with a sharp knife or skewer.

2 Meanwhile, lightly poach the salmon fillet in a saucepan of gently simmering water for 4–5 minutes (if in one piece), or until just cooked but still moist. Alternatively, cut into 2–3 evenly sized pieces and cook in a microwave oven on Medium for 2 minutes, then turn the pieces around so that the cooked parts are in the centre, and cook for a further 1 minute, or until just cooked but still moist. Using a fork, flake the flesh into a bowl.

3 In a separate bowl, blend the soft cheese with just enough of the milk to loosen, then stir in the herbs and a little salt and pepper.

4 When the potatoes are cooked, preheat the grill to high. Cut the potatoes in half lengthways. Carefully scoop the potato flesh out of the skins, reserving the skins, add to the soft cheese mixture and mash together. Lightly stir in the salmon flakes.

5 Spoon the filling into the potato skins and top with the Cheddar cheese. Cook under the preheated grill for 1–2 minutes until the cheese is bubbling and turning golden. Serve immediately.

Cook's Tip
* Pregnant women should avoid using unpasteurised cream cheese or mould-ripened cheeses such as Brie in this recipe.

Eggs and Peppers on Toast

> **NUTRITION NOTES** This dish is an excellent source of choline, vitamins B12, E and folate, and also a good source of vitamins B6, C and E, and carotene.

SERVES 4 Ⓓ Ⓟ Ⓒ (see Cook's Tips), Ⓥ Ⓛ
2 tbsp olive oil
2 large red peppers, deseeded and chopped
1 small red onion, very finely chopped
pinch of paprika, plus extra to garnish (optional)
4 slices dark rye bread
8 large organic eggs
4 tbsp skimmed milk
salt and pepper

1 Heat half the oil in a non-stick frying pan over a medium-high heat, add the red peppers and onion and cook, stirring frequently, for 10 minutes, or until soft. Add the paprika, stir and set aside.

2 Toast one side of the bread slices. Brush the other sides with 1 tablespoon of the remaining oil, then lightly toast. Keep warm.

3 Beat the eggs with the milk and a little salt and pepper to taste in a bowl. Brush the remaining oil over the base of a non-stick saucepan, add the egg mixture and cook over a medium-high heat, stirring frequently to make sure that the eggs don't stick, for 5 minutes, or until cooked to your liking.

4 Gently stir in the red pepper mixture, then spoon onto the rye toasts. Sprinkle with a little extra paprika to garnish, if you like, and serve immediately.

Cook's Tips
* For young children, the ill, pregnant or elderly, ensure that the eggs are thoroughly cooked rather than soft/runny.
* You can buy rye bread in most delicatessens, speciality shops and major supermarkets.

Quick Smoked Mackerel Pâté

> **NUTRITION NOTES** This pâté is a good source of omega-3 fatty acids, vitamins B6 and B12, and selenium.

SERVES 4 Ⓓ Ⓟ Ⓒ (aged over 1 year), Ⓥ Ⓛ
300 g/10¹/₂ oz smoked mackerel fillets
200 ml/7 fl oz natural 8 per cent-fat fromage frais
2 tsp horseradish sauce
juice of ¹/₂ lemon
1 tbsp chopped fresh parsley
pepper
oat cakes, toasted rye bread or wholemeal pitta bread, to serve

1 Flake the mackerel flesh off the skin into a bowl. Add all the remaining ingredients and mash together. Season to taste with pepper. Cover and chill in the refrigerator for 1 hour.

2 Serve the pâté with oat cakes.

Cook's Tip
* Smoked mackerel is quite high in salt, so avoid giving this pâté to small children, unless the rest of the day's diet is very low in salt.

Variation
* You can use Greek-style yogurt instead of the fromage frais.

Main Courses – Fish and Seafood

Our selection of tasty fish and seafood recipes includes several which are not only high in omega-3, but also rich in a variety of other 'brain food' nutrients. Whether you are looking for a very quick and easy supper or a dinner party dish, there is plenty to choose from. Try to buy the freshest fish you can for maximum taste and best texture.

KEY
Ⓥ Suitable for vegetarians
Ⓓ Ideal for weight control
Ⓟ Suitable for pregnancy
Ⓒ Suitable for children
Ⓠ Quick to prepare and cook
Ⓛ Low cost

Thai Swordfish Kebabs

> **NUTRITION NOTES** These kebabs are a good source of omega-3 fatty acids, l-tyrosine, selenium, vitamin B12, vitamin C and antioxidants.

SERVES 4 Ⓓ Ⓠ
700 g/1 lb 9 oz swordfish steaks, cut into bite-sized chunks
2 red peppers, deseeded and cut into bite-sized squares
1 red onion, cut into bite-sized chunks
2 limes
2 garlic cloves, finely chopped
2 tsp chopped fresh root ginger
2 red chillies, deseeded and finely chopped
1 tsp dried lemon grass
2 tbsp sesame oil
1 handful fresh coriander leaves

1 Put the swordfish, red peppers and onion in a non-metallic dish. Finely grate the rind (without pith) from one of the limes and add to the dish, then squeeze the juice from both limes and add to the dish along with all the remaining ingredients. Stir well, cover and leave to marinate in a cool place for 30 minutes–1 hour, if possible.

2 Preheat the grill or a gas barbecue to high, or prepare a charcoal barbecue. Thread the swordfish, red peppers and onion alternately onto 4 metal kebab sticks (or wooden kebab sticks, presoaked in cold water for 30 minutes). Cook the kebabs under the grill or over the barbecue for 8 minutes, turning halfway through and spooning any remaining marinade over as you do so. Serve immediately.

Cook's Tips
* Put the fish in the refrigerator if leaving for more than 30 minutes to marinate.
* The kebabs are great served with rice and a herby side salad.

Variations
* You can choose monkfish, halibut or other firm-fleshed fish for this recipe. If using any fish other than swordfish, shark or marlin, this recipe will be suitable for children under 16 and pregnant women.
* Choose mild or hot chillies, according to preference.

Swordfish Steaks with Lemon Dressing

> **NUTRITION NOTES** This dish is a good source of omega-3 fatty acids, l-tyrosine, vitamin B12, selenium and antioxidants.

SERVES 4 Ⓓ Ⓠ
5 tbsp olive oil, plus extra for brushing
juice of ¹/₂ large or 1 small lemon
2 garlic cloves, well crushed
2 tsp finely chopped fresh oregano
2 tbsp chopped fresh parsley
4 swordfish steaks, about 175 g/6 oz each
salt and pepper

1 Put all the ingredients, except the swordfish, with a little salt and pepper to taste, in a screw-top jar and shake well to combine.

2 Preheat a ridged griddle pan over a high heat. Pat the swordfish steaks dry with kitchen paper and lightly brush with oil on both sides. When the griddle pan is very hot, add the swordfish steaks and cook for 2 minutes on each side, or until cooked through but still moist inside.

3 Serve the swordfish immediately, with the lemon dressing drizzled over – shake it again before drizzling.

Cook's Tips
* This dish is good served with new potatoes and green vegetables such as broccoli or asparagus, or a salad.
* Instead of griddling the swordfish, you can simply grill it or cook it in a non-stick frying pan.
* If you can't find fresh oregano, use 1 teaspoon dried oregano.

Variation
* This recipe also works well with sea bass and halibut. If not using swordfish, marlin or shark, this recipe is suitable for children under 16 and pregnant women.

Spiced Mackerel with Tomato Salad

> **NUTRITION NOTES** This is an excellent source of omega-3 fatty acids, carotene, vitamin C, B6 and B12, selenium and antioxidants.

SERVES 4 Ⓓ Ⓟ Ⓒ Ⓠ Ⓛ
4 garlic cloves, well crushed
finely grated zest and juice of 1 lemon
1 heaped tsp ground cumin
1 heaped tsp smoked paprika
2–3 tbsp olive oil
4 large mackerel fillets, about 200 g/7 oz each, or 8 small, about 100 g/3½ oz each

TOMATO SALAD
300 g/10½ oz juicy ripe tomatoes
1 small red onion, thinly sliced
1 heaped tbsp chopped fresh herbs, such as thyme, mint or parsley
2 tbsp olive oil
1 tbsp white wine vinegar
pinch of caster sugar
salt and pepper

1 Mix the garlic, lemon zest and juice, cumin, paprika and oil together in a small bowl. Put the mackerel fillets in a shallow, non-metallic dish and thoroughly rub both sides with the spice mixture. Cover and leave to marinate in a cool place for 30 minutes, if possible.

2 Preheat the grill to high. Lay the mackerel fillets in the grill pan and cook under the preheated grill for 3 minutes on one side, then turn over, drizzle with any remaining marinade and cook for a further 2–3 minutes, or until the mackerel is cooked through.

3 Meanwhile, prepare the salad. Slice the tomatoes and arrange with the onion on a serving platter. Put the herbs, oil, vinegar, sugar and a little salt and pepper to taste in a screw-top jar and shake well to combine.

4 Drizzle the dressing over the salad and serve with the hot mackerel fillets.

Tuna Steaks with Catalan Sauce

> **NUTRITION NOTES** This dish is a good source of omega-3 fatty acids, vitamins B6, B12, C and E, carotenes and selenium.

SERVES 4 Ⓓ Ⓟ Ⓒ Ⓠ
2 tbsp olive oil, plus extra for brushing
1 onion, chopped
2 red peppers, deseeded and chopped
1 red chilli, deseeded and chopped
1 garlic clove, chopped
400 g/14 oz canned chopped tomatoes
dash of white wine vinegar
50 g/1¾ oz ground almonds
4 tuna steaks, about 125 g/4½ oz each
salt and pepper

1 Heat the oil in a non-stick frying pan over a medium-high heat, add the onion and red peppers and cook, stirring frequently, for 10 minutes, or until soft. Add the chilli and garlic and cook, stirring, for 1 minute. Add the tomatoes and their juice, bring to a simmer and cook for 15 minutes. Stir in the vinegar.

2 Transfer the tomato mixture to a blender or food processor. Add the ground almonds and blend for 20 seconds, or until smooth. Season with a little salt and pepper to taste, and add a little water if the mixture is too thick to pour.

3 Preheat the grill to high, or heat a frying pan or ridged griddle pan over a high heat. Pat the tuna steaks dry with kitchen paper and lightly brush with oil on both sides. Cook under the preheated grill or in the very hot frying pan or griddle pan for 1 minute on each side to sear, or until cooked to your liking.

4 Serve the tuna steaks immediately on warmed plates, with the sauce spooned around.

Cook's Tip
* Don't overcook tuna, otherwise it will become dry, and don't overblend the sauce, or the almonds will become greasy.

Grilled Salmon with Green Lentils and Caper Sauce

NUTRITION NOTES This dish is rich in omega-3 fatty acids, vitamins B1, B6, B12 and E, folate and selenium.

SERVES 4 ⒹⓅⒸⓁ
175 g/6 oz green lentils
5 tbsp light olive oil
2 tbsp balsamic vinegar
2 spring onions or 1 mild shallot, finely chopped
2 garlic cloves, well crushed
2 tsp smooth Dijon mustard
1 heaped tbsp capers, rinsed
1 tbsp chopped fresh dill
4 salmon steaks or fillets, about 150 g/5^1/$_2$ oz each
salt and pepper
fresh dill sprigs, to garnish

1 Cook the lentils in a saucepan of boiling water for 25 minutes, or until tender.

2 Meanwhile, put all the remaining ingredients, except the salmon, with a little salt and pepper to taste, in a screw-top jar and shake well to combine.

3 When the lentils are cooked, drain, tip into a bowl and mix in the dressing.

4 Preheat the grill to high. Cook the salmon steaks under the preheated grill for 5 minutes, or until cooked through but still moist inside.

5 Serve the salmon steaks immediately on a bed of the dressed lentils, garnished with the dill sprigs.

Cook's Tips
* Buy organic or wild salmon, which tends to have higher levels of the important omega-3 fatty acids.
* This dish is good served with a tomato salad.

Angler's Filo Pie

NUTRITION NOTES This pie is a good source of omega-3 fatty acids, l-tyrosine, choline, vitamin B6, lutein, selenium, zinc and iron.

SERVES 4 Ⓟ Ⓒ (aged over 1 year), Ⓛ

500 g/1 lb 2 oz mixed fish fillets, such as coley, haddock, monkfish, sea bass and/or salmon

600 ml/1 pint skimmed milk

1 small onion, peeled but kept whole

6 black peppercorns

1 heaped tbsp sauce flour or cornflour

1 tsp smooth Dijon mustard

100 g/3½ oz cooked peeled prawns

150 g/5½ oz cooked baby spinach, well drained

2 hard-boiled eggs, shelled and quartered

1 tbsp chopped fresh parsley

6 sheets filo pastry, thawed if frozen

olive oil, for brushing

salt

1 Preheat the oven to 190°C/375°F/Gas Mark 5.

2 Put the fish fillets in a large saucepan with the milk, onion and peppercorns. Bring to a simmer and simmer gently for 4–5 minutes, or until the fish is just cooked. Remove the fish with a fish slice and cut into bite-sized pieces. Remove the peppercorns.

3 Add the sauce flour to the milk and heat over a medium heat, whisking constantly, until the mixture thickens. Stir in the mustard and a little salt to taste. Remove from heat.

4 Arrange the fish, prawns, spinach, eggs and parsley in a baking dish and pour the white sauce evenly over the top.

5 Take the pastry sheets from their pack, quickly gather each one up into folds and place on the pie, side by side but slightly overlapping, until the dish is covered. Brush the top thoroughly with oil.

6 Bake in the preheated oven for 25 minutes, or until the top is golden. Serve immediately.

Cook's Tips
* Sauce flour is useful, as you don't need any fat to make a white sauce – it is available in most supermarkets.
* If the white sauce seems a little thick – it should be a good pouring consistency – just add some hot water and whisk again.
* Try to include some salmon for its omega-3 fatty acids.
* Serve with a selection of vegetables.

Variation
* You can add 2–3 tablespoons of grated Cheddar cheese to the white sauce, if you like.

Salmon Potato Patties with Jalapeño

SERVES 4 Ⓓ Ⓟ Ⓒ Ⓠ Ⓛ

400 g/14 oz potatoes, peeled and cut into medium-sized chunks

400 g/14 oz skinless salmon fillet

2 tbsp mayonnaise

1 egg, beaten

dash of skimmed milk, if needed

2 red jalapeño chillies, deseeded and finely chopped

1 small bunch fresh coriander leaves

plain flour, for dusting

1 tbsp olive oil

salt and pepper

NUTRITION NOTES These patties are a good source of omega-3 fatty acids, B vitamins and vitamin E and selenium, and also contain vitamin C and antioxidants.

1 Cook the potatoes in a large saucepan of lightly salted boiling water for 15 minutes, or until tender.

2 Meanwhile, lightly poach the salmon fillet in a saucepan of gently simmering water for 5–6 minutes (if in one piece), or until just cooked but still moist. Alternatively, cut into 4 evenly sized pieces and cook in a microwave oven on Medium for 3 minutes, then turn the pieces around so that the cooked parts are in the centre, and cook for a further 1–2 minutes – check after 1 minute; the fish should be barely cooked. Using a fork, flake the flesh into a bowl.

3 Drain the potatoes, return to the saucepan (if a colander is used to drain) and, while still warm, roughly mash with a fork, adding the mayonnaise, egg and milk, if needed – the mixture must remain firm, so add only if necessary and only a little. Stir in the chillies, coriander leaves and a little salt and pepper to taste, then lightly mix in the salmon flakes.

4 With floured hands, form the mixture into 8 small patties. Heat the oil in a large, non-stick frying pan over a medium-high heat, add the patties and cook for 5 minutes on each side, or until golden brown. Carefully remove with a fish slice and serve immediately.

Cook's Tips

* You can use any mild chillies, but they have to be fresh.

* Serve with an avocado salad or a selection of green vegetables.

Red Mullet Parcels with Olives

> **NUTRITION NOTES** These parcels offer a reasonable source of omega-3 fatty acids and a good source of l-tyrosine, magnesium, selenium, vitamins C and E, carotene and antioxidants.

SERVES 4 ⒹⓅⒸⓆ
4 red mullet, about 275 g/9³/₄ oz each, cleaned and scaled
2 tbsp olive oil
1 heaped tbsp sun-dried tomato paste
2 beef tomatoes, thickly sliced
12 stoned black olives, halved
1 heaped tbsp chopped fresh flat-leaf parsley or basil
pepper
lemon or lime wedges, to serve

1 Preheat the oven to 180°C/350°F/Gas Mark 4.

2 Lay each fish on an individual sheet of non-stick baking paper. Mix the oil and sun-dried tomato paste together in a small bowl, then spoon the mixture over the fish.

3 Arrange the tomato slices and olive halves over the top and then scatter over the herbs and season to taste with pepper.

4 Fold up each sheet of baking paper to enclose the ingredients securely, leaving an air pocket over each fish. Transfer the parcels to a baking sheet and bake in the centre of the preheated oven for 20 minutes, or until the fish is cooked through.

5 Serve in the parcels, garnished with lemon or lime wedges.

Variations
* You can use any small to medium whole fish.
* You can use red pesto instead of the sun-dried tomato paste.

Baked Sea Bass with White Bean Purée

> **NUTRITION NOTES** This dish is a good source of omega-3 fatty acids, l-tyrosine, vitamins B1, B6 and C, folate, iron, magnesium, selenium, carotene and antioxidants.

SERVES 4 ⒹⓅⒸⓆ
2 tbsp olive oil
1 tbsp fresh thyme leaves
4 large sea bass fillets, about 175 g/6 oz each
cherry tomatoes on the vine, to serve
salt and pepper

WHITE BEAN PURÉE
3 tbsp olive oil
2 garlic cloves, chopped
800 g/1 lb 12 oz canned cannellini or butter beans, drained and rinsed
juice of 1 lemon
2–3 tbsp water
4 tbsp chopped fresh flat-leaf parsley

1 Preheat the oven to 200°C/400°F/Gas Mark 6. Mix the oil, thyme and a little salt and pepper to taste together in a small bowl or jug. Arrange the sea bass fillets on a baking tray, pour over the oil mixture and carefully turn to coat well. Put the tray on the top shelf of the preheated oven and bake for 15 minutes.

2 Meanwhile, make the bean purée. Heat the oil in a saucepan over a medium heat, add the garlic and cook, stirring, for 1 minute. Add the beans and heat through for 3–4 minutes, then add the lemon juice and a little salt and pepper to taste. Transfer to a blender or food processor, add the water and blend lightly until you have a purée. Alternatively, mash thoroughly with a fork. Stir the parsley into the purée.

3 Serve the sea bass fillets on top of the warm bean purée with a drizzle of any pan juices. Serve with vine tomatoes.

Cook's Tip
* If the fish fillets are thin, they may cook in less than the specified baking time. Check and remove from the oven after 8–10 minutes if necessary. Keep warm while the tomatoes finish cooking.

Seafood Provençale

NUTRITION NOTES This dish is a good source of vitamins B12 and C, magnesium, zinc, selenium and antioxidants, and omega-3 fatty acids.

SERVES 4 Ⓓ Ⓟ © (aged over 5 years), Ⓠ

2 tbsp olive oil
12 raw scallops, shelled, cleaned and halved
1 large onion, finely chopped
2 garlic cloves, well crushed
400 g/14 oz canned chopped tomatoes
2 tsp dried Herbes de Provence
150 ml/5 fl oz dry white wine
1 mild red chilli, deseeded and chopped (optional)
150 g/5 oz cooked shelled mussels
200 g/7 oz large cooked, peeled prawns
pepper
2 tbsp chopped fresh parsley, to serve

1 Heat the oil in a large frying pan over a high heat, add the scallops and cook for 30 seconds on each side to sear. Remove with a fish slice and set aside.

2 Reduce the heat to medium, add the onion and cook for 8–10 minutes, or until soft and just turning golden.

3 Add the garlic and cook, stirring, for 1 minute, then add the tomatoes and their juice, herbs, wine, chilli, if using, and pepper to taste. Bring to a simmer and cook for 20 minutes.

4 Add the mussels and prawns to the frying pan with the scallops and gently simmer for a further 5 minutes.

5 Serve immediately, sprinkled with the parsley.

Cook's Tips
* Clean mussels by scrubbing or scraping the shells and pulling out any beards attached to the mussels. Discard any opened mussels or mussels with broken shells. Also discard any mussels that remain closed after cooking.
* Shellfish is one of the foods likely to cause an allergic reaction in children, but non-allergic children can eat this soup, or you could substitute other fish for the shellfish.

Chinese Herring Fillets

NUTRITION NOTES This dish is an excellent source of omega-3 fatty acids, vitamin B12, selenium and antioxidants.

SERVES 4 Ⓓ Ⓟ © Ⓠ Ⓛ

4 large herring fillets, about 200–225 g/7–8 oz each, or 8 small, about
    100–125 g/3½–4½ oz each
1 tbsp light soy sauce
1 tbsp dry sherry or vermouth
1 tbsp sesame oil
2 spring onions, finely chopped
pinch of soft light brown sugar
2 tsp chopped fresh root ginger
1 red chilli, deseeded and chopped
2 garlic cloves, chopped
1 large handful fresh coriander leaves

1 Put the herring fillets on a heatproof plate that will fit inside a steamer – you may need to cook the fillets in 2 batches if the steamer cannot accommodate a large plate. Put water in the bottom of the steamer and bring to the boil.

2 Meanwhile, mix the remaining ingredients together in a bowl. Spoon the mixture over the herring fillets, put the plate in the steamer, cover and steam for 4–5 minutes, or until the fish is just cooked.

3 Serve the fish immediately, with the spicy juices spooned over.

Variations
* You can use salmon fillets instead of herring fillets.
* Alternatively, you can bake the herring fillets in the spice mixture in non-stick baking paper parcels (if using small fillets, put 2 in each parcel) in the centre of the oven preheated to 180°C/350°F/Gas Mark 4 for 12 minutes, or until cooked through.

Seafood Paella with Saffron Rice

NUTRITION NOTES This paella is a reasonable source of omega-3 fatty acids and also contains choline, vitamins B6, C and E, carotene, selenium, zinc and antioxidants.

SERVES 4 Ⓓ Ⓟ Ⓒ (aged over 5 years)

1 heaped tsp saffron threads

850 ml/1¹/₂ pints hot fish or vegetable stock, plus extra if needed

3 tbsp olive oil

400 g/14 oz monkfish fillet, cut into bite-sized pieces

1 large Spanish onion, roughly chopped

2 red peppers, deseeded and roughly chopped

1 tsp paprika

1 beef tomato, chopped

275 g/9³/₄ oz paella or white long-grain rice

100 g/3¹/₂ oz frozen petits pois, thawed

500 g/1 lb 2 oz live mussels, scrubbed and debearded

150 g/5¹/₂ oz (prepared weight) large raw prawns, peeled and tails left intact

1 Soak the saffron threads in a little of the stock in a jug or small bowl for 15 minutes.

2 Meanwhile, heat half the oil in a large frying pan or paella pan over a high heat, add the monkfish pieces and cook for 1 minute on each side until lightly browned. Remove with a fish slice and set aside.

3 Heat the remaining oil in the frying pan or paella pan over a medium-high heat, add the onion and red peppers and cook, stirring, for 5 minutes, or until softened. Add the paprika and tomato and cook, stirring, for 1–2 minutes, then add the rice and stir to coat well.

4 Add the saffron threads and their soaking liquid, the remaining stock and the petits pois, stir again and bring to a simmer. Cover and leave to simmer gently for 30 minutes.

5 Add the mussels and prawns with the monkfish, mixing in well. Cook for a further 10 minutes, or until the prawns are cooked and the mussels have opened, adding a little more stock if needed.

6 Test a mouthful of rice to make sure that it is tender (cook for a little longer if not quite ready), then serve immediately.

Cook's Tips

* Clean mussels by scrubbing or scraping the shells and pulling out any beards attached to the mussels. Discard any opened mussels or mussels with broken shells. Also discard any closed mussels after cooking.
* Shellfish is one of the foods likely to cause an allergic reaction in children, but non-allergic children can eat this soup, or you could substitute other fish for the shellfish.
* Serve with a plain mixed-leaf side salad.

Variation

* Raw prawns give a great flavour, but you can use ready-cooked, in which case add them for the last 3 minutes of the cooking time only.

Chilli Crab Cakes with Stir-fried Greens

NUTRITION NOTES This dish is a good source of omega-3 fatty acids, zinc, magnesium, vitamin C and antioxidants, and also a source of choline, vitamin B6, selenium and iron.

SERVES 4 Ⓓ Ⓟ Ⓒ Ⓠ Ⓛ

350 g/12 oz potatoes, peeled and cut into medium-sized chunks
2 tbsp skimmed milk
400 g/14 oz dressed fresh crabmeat
2 tbsp chopped fresh coriander
2 hot green chillies, deseeded and finely chopped
4 spring onions, finely chopped
finely grated rind and juice of 1 lime
2 eggs, beaten
about 3 tbsp plain flour, plus extra for dusting
150 g/5¹/₂ oz slightly stale white or wholemeal breadcrumbs
2 tbsp groundnut oil
selection of oriental greens, such as pak choi, mizuna and
   Chinese leaves
salt

1 Cook the potatoes in a large saucepan of lightly salted water for 15 minutes, or until tender. Drain, return to the saucepan (if a colander used to drain) and mash with the milk.

2 Put the mashed potatoes, crabmeat, coriander, chillies, spring onions, lime rind and juice and half the egg in a large bowl and mix together well with a fork. With floured hands, form the mixture into 8 cakes.

3 Put the flour, remaining egg and breadcrumbs into 3 separate shallow dishes. Coat each cake first in the flour, then in the egg and finally in the breadcrumbs.

4 Heat half the oil in a large, non-stick frying pan over a medium-high heat, add the crab cakes and cook for 4 minutes on each side, or until golden brown. Remove and drain on kitchen paper.

5 Meanwhile, heat the remaining oil in a separate non-stick frying pan or wok over a high heat, add the greens and stir-fry for 2 minutes. Serve immediately with the crab cakes.

Variations
* You could use canned, drained crabmeat, but it is lower in omega-3 fatty acids and may be high in salt.
* Try serving the crab cakes with a chilli dipping sauce.

Teriyaki Prawns with Cashew Nuts

NUTRITION NOTES This dish is a good source of vitamins B12, C and E, carotene, zinc, magnesium, selenium and antioxidants.

SERVES 4 Ⓓ Ⓟ © (aged over 5 years, because of the salt content), ©

1 tbsp groundnut oil
150 g/5¹/₂ oz mangetout
150 g/5¹/₂ oz baby sweetcorn
1 large orange or yellow pepper, deseeded and thinly sliced
8 spring onions, halved lengthways
2 garlic cloves, well crushed
2-cm/³/₄-inch piece fresh root ginger, peeled and finely chopped
2 tbsp teriyaki marinade
100 g/3¹/₂ oz unsalted cashew nuts
400 g/14 oz large cooked peeled prawns
1 tbsp sesame oil

1 Heat the groundnut oil in a large, non-stick preheated wok or frying pan, add all the vegetables and stir-fry over a high heat for 4 minutes, or until almost tender but still with a bite. Add the garlic and ginger and stir-fry for 1 minute.

2 Add the teriyaki marinade, cashew nuts and prawns and stir-fry for 2 minutes.

3 Serve immediately, with the sesame oil drizzled over.

Cook's Tips
* Serve with wholewheat noodles or basmati rice.
* If you have time, toast the cashew nuts beforehand: heat a non-stick frying pan lightly brushed with groundnut oil over a medium-high heat, add the nuts and cook, turning occasionally, for 5 minutes, or until lightly browned.

Variation
* You can vary the vegetables – courgette slices or broccoli florets work well.

Main Courses –
Vegetarian and Meat

For all meat and poultry lovers, the good news is that you can eat lean cuts of meat 2–3 times a week without feeling guilty. Most meats are an excellent source of 'brain food' vitamins and minerals as well as high-quality protein. Include 1–3 vegetarian meals in your weekly diet (and 2 fish meals from the previous chapter) for a perfect balance. The selection of recipes here will help you to achieve just that.

KEY
Ⓥ Suitable for vegetarians
Ⓦ Ideal for weight control
Ⓟ Suitable for pregnancy
Ⓒ Suitable for children
Ⓠ Quick to prepare and cook
Ⓛ Low cost

Warmly Spiced Vegetable Casserole

> **NUTRITION NOTES** This casserole is an excellent source of choline, vitamins B6, C and E, folate and carotene, and also a good source of selenium, magnesium and iron.

SERVES 4 Ⓥ Ⓓ Ⓟ Ⓒ Ⓠ Ⓛ

2 tbsp olive oil

1 large onion, chopped

1 large leek, sliced

2 garlic cloves, chopped

1 small butternut squash, deseeded and cubed

2 carrots, sliced

100 g/3½ oz shredded spring cabbage

400 g/14 oz canned chopped tomatoes

100 g/3½ oz brown or green lentils

250 g/9 oz frozen fresh soya beans, thawed

300 ml/10 fl oz vegetable stock

1–2 tsp garam masala

salt and pepper

2 tbsp chopped fresh parsley, to garnish

1 Heat the oil in a large, flameproof casserole over a medium heat, add the onion and leek and cook, stirring frequently, for 5 minutes, or until softened. Add the garlic, squash and carrots and cook, stirring, for 1 minute.

2 Add the cabbage, tomatoes and their juice, lentils, soya beans and stock, stir well and bring to a simmer. Cover and gently simmer on the hob for 1 hour. Alternatively, transfer to the oven preheated to 160°C/325°F/Gas Mark 3 and cook for 1 hour. Stir halfway through and check that there is still some liquid left in the casserole.

3 Stir in the garam masala and a little salt and pepper to taste 10 minutes before the end of the cooking time. Serve the casserole with the parsley sprinkled over.

Cook's Tips

* You can buy frozen fresh (green) soya beans in packs from the frozen vegetable counter at major supermarkets.
* Garam masala is a mild spice mix containing cumin, coriander and other spices. As an alternative, you could use 1 teaspoon ground cumin and 1 teaspoon ground coriander.

Ratatouille with Poached Eggs

> **NUTRITION NOTES** This dish is an excellent source of choline, vitamins B12, C and E, folate, carotene and antioxidants.

SERVES 4 Ⓥ Ⓓ Ⓠ Ⓛ

2 tbsp olive oil

1 large Spanish onion, sliced

2 peppers, any colour, deseeded and thinly sliced

2 courgettes, sliced into thin rounds

1 small aubergine, halved lengthways and thinly sliced

2 garlic cloves, chopped

300 ml/10 fl oz passata with herbs, plus extra if needed (optional)

2 tsp smoked paprika

8 small eggs

salt and pepper

1 Heat the oil in a large, lidded, non-stick frying pan or shallow, flameproof casserole over a medium-high heat, add the onion and peppers and cook, stirring frequently, for 4–5 minutes until beginning to soften.

2 Add the courgettes, aubergine and garlic and cook, stirring, for 2 minutes. Add the passata, most of the paprika and a little salt and pepper to taste. Stir and bring to a simmer. Reduce the heat to low, cover and leave to simmer gently for 45 minutes, adding a little extra passata or water if the mixture begins to look dry.

3 Make 8 wells in the ratatouille and break an egg into each. Re-cover and cook for a further 10 minutes, or until the egg whites are cooked but the yolks still runny.

4 Serve immediately, garnished with paprika.

Cook's Tips

* Passata is widely available in supermarkets in jars or cartons, usually near to the canned tomatoes, but if you can't find it, use 400 g/14 oz canned chopped tomatoes with herbs instead.
* Lightly cooked eggs should not be served to young children, or the ill, pregnant or elderly.

Traditional Spanish Omelette with Herb Salad

NUTRITION NOTES This dish is an excellent source of choline, vitamin B12 and folate, and a good source of vitamin E.

SERVES 4 Ⓥ Ⓓ Ⓟ Ⓒ (aged over 1 year), Ⓠ Ⓛ

500 g/1 lb 2 oz salad or waxy new potatoes, peeled and cut into
  1-cm/¹/₂-inch rounds
1 tbsp groundnut or light olive oil
2 Spanish onions, thinly sliced
8 eggs
200 g/7 oz mixed salad leaves with herbs
4 tbsp olive oil
1 tbsp lemon juice
salt and pepper

1 Cook the potatoes in a large saucepan of boiling water for 5 minutes, or until just tender. Drain and set aside.

2 Heat the groundnut oil in a large, non-stick frying pan over a medium-high heat, add the onions and cook, stirring frequently, for 10–15 minutes until thoroughly soft and just turning golden. Reduce the heat to medium-low. Arrange the potatoes in the frying pan among the onions, spreading everything evenly over the base.

3 Put the eggs in a bowl with a little cold water and salt and pepper to taste and beat together. Pour the egg mixture evenly over the vegetables in the frying pan. Cook, without stirring, for 5 minutes, or until the underside of the omelette is cooked and golden but the top is still runny. Meanwhile, preheat the grill to high.

4 Put the frying pan under the preheated grill and cook the omelette for 2 minutes, or until the top is cooked and golden. Meanwhile, toss the salad leaves and herbs with the olive oil and lemon juice in a salad bowl.

5 Cut the omelette into 4 wedges and serve with the herb salad.

Cook's Tips
* For young children, the ill, pregnant and elderly, ensure that the omelette is thoroughly cooked in the centre.
* Any leftover omelette is delicious served cold.

Red Pepper Felafel with Hummus Dressing

SERVES 4 Ⓥ Ⓓ Ⓟ Ⓒ Ⓞ Ⓛ

800 g/1 lb 12 oz canned chickpeas, drained and rinsed

2 bottled or canned red peppers, drained and finely chopped

2 shallots, very finely chopped

2 garlic cloves, well crushed

2 tbsp chopped fresh coriander leaves

1 egg, beaten

gram (chickpea) flour, for dusting

1 tbsp olive oil

salt and pepper

HUMMUS DRESSING

1 heaped tbsp hummus

4 tbsp olive oil

1 tbsp lemon juice

2 ripe tomatoes, deseeded and finely chopped

> **NUTRITION NOTES** This dish is an excellent source of folate, vitamin E and iron, and a good source of vitamin C, carotene and antioxidants.

1 Put the chickpeas in a bowl and mash thoroughly with a fork. Add the red peppers, shallots, garlic, coriander, egg and a little salt and pepper to taste and mix well.

2 Dust your hands with the gram flour and form the mixture into 8 small patties. Dust the patties with gram flour.

3 Heat the oil in a large, non-stick frying pan over a medium heat, add the patties and cook, turning occasionally, for 8 minutes, or until golden brown.

4 Meanwhile, beat all the ingredients for the dressing together in a small bowl.

5 Serve the felafel hot, with the dressing spooned around.

Cook's Tips

* You can buy gram (chickpea) flour from health-food shops or in the health-food section of the supermarket. Alternatively, you can use ordinary plain flour.

* Felafel are great served with a bulgar wheat and cucumber salad.

Sweet Chilli Chicken with Creole Rice

SERVES 4 ⒹⓅⒸⓁ

8 skinless, boneless chicken thighs, about 100 g/3¹/₂ oz each

2 tbsp sweet chilli dipping sauce

2 tbsp orange juice

2 garlic cloves, well crushed

salt and pepper

CREOLE RICE

600 ml/1 pint water

250 g/9 oz white long-grain rice

1 tbsp olive oil

1 large red pepper, deseeded and finely chopped

1 small onion, finely chopped

1 tsp paprika

400 g/14 oz canned mixed beans, drained and rinsed

1 Put the chicken in a shallow, non-metallic bowl. Mix the chilli sauce, orange juice, garlic and a little salt and pepper to taste together in a small bowl and spoon over the chicken. Using your hands, coat the chicken thighs thoroughly in the marinade. Cover and leave to marinate in the refrigerator for 1–2 hours.

2 Preheat the oven to 180°C/350°F/Gas Mark 4. Transfer the chicken thighs to a non-stick baking tray and bake in the preheated oven, turning halfway through, for 25 minutes, or until tender and the juices run clear when a skewer is inserted into the thickest part of the meat.

3 Meanwhile, make the rice. Lightly salt the water and bring to the boil in a saucepan. Add the rice and stir well. Cover, reduce the heat to low and leave to simmer, undisturbed, for 15 minutes, or until tender and all the water has been absorbed.

4 While the rice is cooking, heat the oil in a non-stick frying pan over a medium-high heat, add the pepper and onion and cook, stirring frequently, for 10–15 minutes, or until the onion is thoroughly soft and turning golden, adding the paprika for the last 5 minutes of the cooking time. Stir in the beans and cook for a further 1 minute.

5 Stir the bean mixture into the rice, then serve immediately with the baked chicken.

NUTRITION NOTES This dish is a good source of vitamins B6 and E, folate and selenium, and is also a source of l-tyrosine, zinc, iron and vitamins B12 and C.

Cook's Tips

* Check the rice towards the end of the cooking time – if the water has all been absorbed before the rice is tender, add a little more boiling water to the pan and stir with a fork.
* Serve with a green salad.

Tray-baked Lamb Steaks with Tomatoes

> **NUTRITION NOTES** This dish is an excellent source of l-tyrosine, vitamins B6, B12, C and E, iron, zinc, selenium and antioxidants.

SERVES 4 Ⓓ Ⓟ Ⓒ Ⓛ

2 beef tomatoes, cut into thick slices
2 red onions, each cut into 6 wedges
4 large garlic cloves, peeled
1 tsp sea salt
3 tbsp olive oil, plus extra for brushing
1 heaped tsp dried Herbes de Provence
4 lamb steaks, about 175 g/6 oz each
pepper

TO SERVE

4 wholemeal pitta breads
50 g/1³/₄ oz pine kernels, toasted
1 handful fresh basil leaves
200 ml/7 fl oz thick natural yogurt

1 Preheat the oven to 190°C/375°F/Gas Mark 5. Arrange the tomato slices and onion wedges in a roasting tin. Put the garlic cloves and salt in a mortar and crush to a purée with a pestle. Work in the oil. Spoon the mixture over the vegetables and mix well. Sprinkle over the herbs and season to taste with pepper. Put on the top shelf of the preheated oven and roast for 20 minutes.

2 Meanwhile, lightly brush the lamb steaks with oil. Heat a non-stick frying pan over a high heat. When very hot, add the lamb steaks and cook for 1 minute on each side to sear.

3 Remove the roasting tin from the oven. Turn the vegetables over, arrange the lamb steaks on top and spoon over the juices from the corners of the tin, adding a little water if too dry. Return the tin to the oven and roast for a further 15–20 minutes until the vegetables are tender and the lamb is cooked to your liking. Sprinkle the pitta breads with water and put them in the oven for the last 1–2 minutes of the cooking time.

4 Scatter the pine kernels and basil over the lamb and vegetables before serving, adding a portion of yogurt and a warmed pitta bread to each plate.

Spicy Chicken with Tortilla Wrap

> **NUTRITION NOTES** This dish is an excellent source of vitamins B6, C and E, carotene and selenium, and is also a source of folate and antioxidants.

SERVES 4 Ⓓ Ⓟ Ⓒ Ⓠ Ⓛ

2 tbsp olive oil, plus extra if needed
juice of 1 lime
2 tsp fajita seasoning
3 skinless, boneless chicken breasts, about 150 g/5¹/₂ oz each
1 red onion, thinly sliced
2 yellow peppers, deseeded and thinly sliced
3 ripe tomatoes, sliced
1 large ripe avocado
4 large tortilla wraps
4 tbsp thick natural yogurt

1 Put the oil, lime juice and fajita seasoning in a shallow, non-metallic bowl. Slice the chicken into thin strips, add to the bowl and toss to coat well. Cover and leave to marinate in a cool place for 30 minutes.

2 Heat a non-stick frying pan over a high heat, add the chicken and its marinade, the onion and yellow peppers and cook, stirring, for 3 minutes. Add the tomatoes and cook, stirring, for 2 minutes, adding a little more oil if the frying pan seems too dry. Remove from the heat.

3 Peel, stone and slice the avocado. Warm the wraps according to the packet instructions. Divide the chicken mixture between the wraps, spooning it into the centre of each. Add a quarter of the avocado and a tablespoonful of yogurt to each filling and wrap up.

4 Serve the wraps immediately.

Variations

* You can add a handful of fresh coriander leaves to the tortillas before wrapping.
* For vegetarians, use firm tofu instead of the chicken.

Lamb Kebabs with Greek Salad

NUTRITION NOTES This dish is an excellent source of l-tyrosine, vitamins B6 and B12, iron and zinc, and a good source of vitamin C, carotene and antioxidants.

SERVES 4 Ⓓ Ⓟ Ⓒ Ⓛ

800 g/1 lb 12 oz lamb leg fillet, cut into large bite-sized cubes

2 tbsp olive oil

juice of ¹/₂ lemon

2 garlic cloves, very finely chopped

1 tbsp chopped fresh oregano or 1 heaped tsp dried

salt and pepper

GREEK SALAD

3 tomatoes

1 small red onion, thinly sliced

8-cm/3¹/₄-inch piece cucumber, roughly chopped

8 cos lettuce leaves, torn

100 g/3¹/₂ oz feta cheese (drained weight), crumbled

8 stoned black olives

olive oil, for drizzling

lemon, for squeezing

1 Put the lamb cubes into a shallow, non-metallic bowl. Mix the oil, lemon juice, garlic, oregano and a little salt and pepper to taste together in a small bowl, spoon over the lamb and turn to coat thoroughly. Cover and leave to marinate in the refrigerator for 1–2 hours, or preferably overnight or up to 8 hours.

2 Preheat the grill to high. Thread the lamb onto 4 metal kebab sticks (or wooden kebab sticks, presoaked in cold water for 30 minutes). Cook the kebabs under the preheated grill, turning halfway through and spooning over any remaining marinade, for 8–10 minutes, or until the lamb is browned but pink inside.

3 Meanwhile, make the salad. Arrange all the vegetables on serving plates and top with the feta cheese and olives. Drizzle over the oil and add a squeeze of lemon juice. Season with a little salt and pepper to taste. Add a kebab to each plate and serve immediately.

Variation

* You could use pork fillet in place of the lamb.

Turkish Lamb Casserole

NUTRITION NOTES This casserole is an excellent source of l-tyrosine, vitamins B6, B12 and C, iron and zinc, and a good source of carotene, folate, vitamin E and antioxidants.

SERVES 4 Ⓓ Ⓟ Ⓒ Ⓛ

2 tbsp olive oil

4 lamb shanks, about 300 g/10¹/₂ oz each

2 onions, sliced

2 peppers, any colour, deseeded and chopped

2 garlic cloves, well crushed

1 aubergine, cut into small cubes

¹/₂ tsp paprika

¹/₂ tsp ground cinnamon

200 g/7 oz cooked chickpeas

400 g/14 oz canned chopped tomatoes

2 tsp mixed dried Mediterranean herbs

100 ml/3¹/₂ fl oz lamb or vegetable stock, plus extra if needed

salt and pepper

1 Preheat the oven to 160°C/325°F/Gas Mark 3. Heat half the oil in a large, non-stick frying pan over a high heat, add the lamb shanks and cook, turning frequently, for 2–3 minutes until browned all over. Transfer to a casserole.

2 Heat the remaining oil in the frying pan over a medium-high heat, add the onions and peppers and cook, stirring frequently, for 10–15 minutes, or until the onions are thoroughly soft and just turning golden. Add the garlic, aubergine and spices and cook, stirring constantly, for 1 minute. Add the chickpeas, tomatoes and their juice, herbs and enough stock to cover the base of the frying pan by about 2 cm/3/4 inch, stir well and bring to a simmer. Season with a little salt and pepper to taste and transfer to a casserole.

3 Cover the casserole, transfer to the middle shelf of the preheated oven and cook for 1 hour. Check after 45 minutes that the casserole is gently bubbling and that there is enough liquid – if it looks rather dry, add a little more stock or boiling water and stir in. If bubbling too much, reduce the oven temperature.

Cook's Tip

* The casserole is good served with rice, couscous or bulgar wheat.

Chilli Beef with Avocado Salsa

NUTRITION NOTES This dish is an excellent source of l-tyrosine, vitamins B6, B12, C and E, folate, iron, and zinc, and is also a good source of carotene.

SERVES 4 Ⓓ Ⓟ Ⓒ Ⓛ
2 tbsp olive oil
1 large onion, finely chopped
2 green peppers, deseeded and finely chopped
2 garlic cloves, finely chopped
2 tsp hot chilli paste or powder, or to taste
400 g/14 oz fresh lean beef mince
400 g/14 oz canned chopped tomatoes with herbs
1 tbsp sun-dried tomato paste
200 g/7 oz canned red kidney beans, drained and rinsed
salt and pepper

AVOCADO SALSA
1 large or 2 small ripe avocados
1 small red onion, finely chopped
juice of $\frac{1}{2}$ lime
1 tomato, deseeded and finely chopped
1 small handful fresh coriander leaves
4 tbsp thick natural yogurt

1 Heat the oil in a large, non-stick, lidded frying pan over a medium-high heat, add the onion and green peppers and cook, stirring frequently, for 10 minutes, or until soft. Add the garlic and cook, stirring, for 1 minute, then add the chilli paste and stir again.

2 Push all the vegetables to the side of the frying pan, add the mince to the centre and cook, breaking it up with a wooden spoon and stirring, for 5 minutes, or until browned all over. Stir the vegetables into the mince.

3 Add the tomatoes and their juice and tomato paste and stir well to combine. Stir in the beans. Bring to a slow simmer, cover and cook for 1 hour. Add a little salt and pepper to taste.

4 When the chilli is nearly cooked, make the salsa. Peel, stone and chop the avocado. Put in a bowl with the remaining ingredients and stir to combine.

5 Serve the chilli hot with the avocado salsa.

Cook's Tips
* Taste the chilli towards the end of cooking time, and if it isn't hot enough for you, add a few drops of Tabasco sauce. You can use fresh chillies instead, in which case the amount will depend on the strength of the chilli and your own tastes, but 2–4 fresh chillies should suffice. Fresh chillies are milder than dried ones.
* Serve the chilli and salsa with baked potatoes, rice or flatbreads.

Hoisin Beef with Mushrooms

NUTRITION NOTES This dish is an excellent source of l-tyrosine, vitamins B6 and B12, folate, zinc, iron and antioxidants.

SERVES 4 © (aged over 4 years, because of the salt content), ⓠ ⓛ

500 g/1 lb 2 oz lean beef steak, such as fillet or rump

2 tbsp groundnut oil

200 g/7 oz shiitake or chestnut mushrooms

2 courgettes, thinly sliced

2 large garlic cloves, well crushed

2 tsp finely chopped fresh root ginger

2 tbsp hoisin sauce

2 tsp sesame oil

about 4 tbsp beef stock

1 Cut the beef into thin strips. Heat half the groundnut oil in a large, non-stick frying pan or wok over a high heat, add the beef and cook, turning once or twice, for 2 minutes, until browned all over. Remove with a slotted spoon and set aside.

2 Add the remaining groundnut oil to the frying pan with the mushrooms and courgettes and stir-fry for 3 minutes. Add the garlic and ginger and stir-fry for a further 1 minute.

3 Return the beef to the frying pan, add the hoisin sauce and the sesame oil and cook, stirring, for 1 minute. Add the stock and stir well.

4 Serve immediately.

Cook's Tip
* Serve with rice or noodles.

Variation
* You can use pork fillet instead of the beef.

Beef Satay with Peanut Sauce

NUTRITION NOTES This dish is an excellent source of l-tyrosine, vitamins B12, iron and zinc, a good source of vitamin E and a useful source of vitamin C and carotene.

SERVES 4 © (aged over 5 years, because of the nut pieces), ⓠ ⓛ

600 g/1 lb 5 oz lean beef steak, such as fillet or rump, cut into bite-sized cubes

2 tbsp light soy sauce

1 heaped tsp Thai seasoning

juice of 1 lime

STIR-FRY

1 tbsp sesame oil

2 carrots, cut into batons

8 spring onions, halved lengthways

2 celery sticks, cut into thin 6-cm/2¹/₂-inch lengths

PEANUT SAUCE

3 tbsp chunky peanut butter

2 tbsp canned reduced-fat coconut milk

1 large garlic clove, very well crushed

1 tbsp sweet chilli dipping sauce

1 Put the beef in a non-metallic dish. Mix the soy sauce, seasoning and lime juice in a bowl, spoon over the beef and turn to coat. Cover and marinate in the refrigerator for 1–3 hours. Presoak 8 small wooden kebab sticks in cold water for 30 minutes.

2 Preheat the grill to high. Thread the beef onto the kebab sticks and arrange on the grill rack. Cook for 3 minutes. Turn, baste with any remaining marinade and cook for a further 3 minutes.

3 Meanwhile, make the peanut sauce. Combine all the ingredients for the sauce in a small, non-stick saucepan and heat through, stirring occasionally, over a low heat. Keep warm.

4 To make the stir-fry, heat the oil in a non-stick frying pan or wok over a high heat, add the vegetables and stir-fry for 3–4 minutes.

5 Serve the beef kebabs hot with the sauce and vegetables.

Children's Food

While most of the recipes in this book are suitable for children, this little collection is particularly well received by the majority of kids, from weaning right through to their teens. Even if they say they don't like fish or vegetables, for example, we are confident that they will enjoy these dishes! And of course, each one is rich in foods that will help them to maximise brain power.

For parents who may like to eat with their children, we have included the symbols below in this section.

KEY

Ⓥ Suitable for vegetarians

Ⓦ Ideal for weight control

Ⓟ Suitable for pregnancy

Ⓒ Suitable for children

Ⓠ Quick to prepare and cook

Ⓛ Low cost

Creamy Salmon Pasta

NUTRITION NOTES This pasta dish is a good source of omega-3 fatty acids, vitamins B1, B2, B6, B12 and E, selenium and magnesium.

SERVES 4 CHILDREN Ⓓ Ⓟ Ⓒ Ⓠ Ⓛ

250 g/9 oz dried pasta spirals (wholewheat if preferred)
200 g/7 oz broccoli, broken into small florets
250 g/9 oz skinless salmon fillet
100 g/3¹/₂ oz natural fromage frais
2 tbsp skimmed or semi-skimmed milk
4 tbsp freshly grated Parmesan cheese
2 tsp smooth Dijon mustard
pepper
2 tbsp chopped fresh parsley, to garnish

1 Cook the pasta in a large saucepan of lightly salted boiling water for 20 minutes, or according to the packet instructions, until al dente. Add the broccoli to the saucepan for the last 4 minutes of the cooking time.

2 Meanwhile, lightly poach the salmon fillet in a saucepan of gently simmering water for 4–5 minutes (if in one piece), or until just cooked but still moist. Alternatively, cut into 2–3 evenly sized pieces and cook in a microwave oven on Medium for 2 minutes, then turn the pieces around so that the cooked parts are in the centre, and cook for a further 1 minute, or until just cooked but still moist. Using a fork, flake the flesh into a bowl.

3 Put the fromage frais, milk, Parmesan cheese, mustard and pepper to taste in a separate bowl and beat together.

4 When the pasta and broccoli are cooked, drain and toss with the salmon flakes and the cheese sauce. Serve immediately, garnished with the parsley.

Cook's Tip
* You can put the broccoli in a colander over the pasta to steam, if you prefer.

Variation
* You can also add 100 g/3¹/₂ oz cooked petits pois, if you like.

Real Fish Nuggets

NUTRITION NOTES These nuggets are a good source of vitamins B6 and B12 and selenium, and also a source of iron, zinc, vitamin E and antioxidants. If salmon is used, it is also a good source of omega-3 fatty acids.

SERVES 4 CHILDREN Ⓓ Ⓟ Ⓒ Ⓠ Ⓛ

400 g/14 oz firm fish fillets, such as monkfish, haddock, cod, hake or salmon
2 tbsp plain flour
1 tsp mild paprika
2 tsp very finely chopped fresh parsley
1 egg, beaten
75 g/2³/₄ oz fresh wholemeal breadcrumbs
1 tbsp light olive oil
salt and pepper

1 Cut the fish fillets into bite-sized chunks. Put the flour, paprika, parsley and a very little salt and pepper to taste in a bowl and mix together.

2 Put the seasoned flour, egg and breadcrumbs into 3 separate shallow dishes. Coat each nugget first in the flour, then in the egg and finally in the breadcrumbs.

3 Heat the oil in a large, non-stick frying pan over a medium-high heat, add the nuggets and cook, turning occasionally, for 7 minutes, or until golden brown all over. Reduce the heat slightly if the nuggets are browning too much, too quickly. Remove and drain on kitchen paper before serving.

Cook's Tip
* Farmed cod is now available, and is a good, eco-friendly substitute for wild cod.

Variation
* You can alternatively bake the nuggets in the oven, preheated to 190°C/375°F/Gas Mark 5. Gently brush with the oil and bake for 15 minutes, turning occasionally.

Tuna Pasta Bake

NUTRITION NOTES This pasta bake is an excellent source of omega-3 fatty acids, carotene, vitamin B6 and B12, selenium, magnesium and l-tyrosine, and also a source of vitamins C and E.

SERVES 4 CHILDREN Ⓓ Ⓟ Ⓒ

1 tbsp olive oil

1 large onion, chopped

1 garlic clove, crushed

400 g/14 oz canned chopped tomatoes with herbs

a few fresh basil leaves

250 g/9 oz dried wholewheat pasta tubes

400 g/14 oz fresh tuna steaks

salt and pepper

CHEESE SAUCE

1 tbsp sauce flour or cornflour

500 ml/18 fl oz skimmed or semi-skimmed milk

100 g/3½ oz mature Cheddar cheese, grated

1 Heat the oil in a large, non-stick frying pan over a medium heat, add the onion and garlic and cook, stirring frequently, for 10 minutes, or until the onion is soft. Add the tomatoes and their juice, basil and a very little salt and pepper to taste. Stir and bring to a simmer. Reduce the heat to low and simmer gently for 20 minutes.

2 Meanwhile, cook the pasta in a large saucepan of lightly salted boiling water for 20 minutes, or according to the packet instructions, until al dente. Drain and keep warm.

3 While the tomato sauce and pasta are cooking, make the cheese sauce. Put the sauce flour and milk in a non-stick saucepan over a medium heat, bring to a simmer and cook, stirring frequently, for 8 minutes, or until the sauce thickens. Add most of the Cheddar cheese and stir well. Preheat the oven to 190°C/375°F/Gas Mark 5.

4 Cut the tuna into small bite-sized pieces, add to the tomato sauce and stir. Leave to cook for 3 minutes.

5 Tip the pasta into a lasagne dish or similar, suitably sized ovenproof dish, pour the tuna and tomato sauce over and combine well. Level the surface, then pour over the cheese sauce. Sprinkle the remaining cheese over the top and bake in the preheated oven for 25 minutes, or until the top is golden and bubbling. Serve immediately.

Cook's Tip

* Sauce flour is a very fine-grade wheat flour widely available in supermarkets. Using it means that you don't need fat to make a smooth white or cheese sauce.

Variation

* You can use salmon instead of the tuna, or even chicken fillets.

Salmon Fish Cakes

NUTRITION NOTES These fish cakes are a good source of omega-3 fatty acids, B vitamins, vitamin E and selenium, and also contain vitamin C and antioxidants.

SERVES 4 CHILDREN ⓓⓟⓒⓞⓛ

300 g/10¹/₂ oz skinless salmon fillet
300 g/10¹/₂ oz firm mashed potatoes
2 tbsp natural fromage frais
1 tbsp chopped fresh parsley
2 tbsp plain flour, plus extra for dusting
1 egg, beaten
75 g/2³/₄ oz fresh wholemeal breadcrumbs
1 tbsp light olive oil
salt and pepper

1 Lightly poach the salmon fillet in a saucepan of gently simmering water for 5 minutes (if in one piece), or until just cooked but still moist. Alternatively, cut into 3–4 evenly sized pieces and cook in a microwave oven on Medium for 2 minutes, then turn the pieces around so that the cooked parts are in the centre, and cook for a further 1–2 minutes – check after 1 minute; the fish should be barely cooked.

2 Using a fork, flake the salmon flesh into a bowl, add the mashed potatoes, fromage frais, parsley and a very little salt and pepper to taste and mix together thoroughly. With floured hands, form the mixture into 4 cakes.

3 Put the flour, egg and breadcrumbs into 3 separate shallow dishes. Coat each cake first in the flour, then in the egg and finally in the breadcrumbs.

4 Heat the oil in a large, non-stick frying pan over a medium-high heat, add the fish cakes and cook for 5 minutes on each side, or until golden brown. Reduce the heat slightly if the cakes are browning too much, too quickly. Remove and drain on kitchen paper before serving.

Cook's Tips
* Serve with peas and lightly cooked tomato halves.
* This is a great dish for using up leftover mashed potatoes. If you have leftover boiled potatoes, just reheat in a microwave oven and mash with a little skimmed milk.

Vegetable Fritters

NUTRITION NOTES These fritters are a good source of vitamins B1, B6 and C, folate, carotene and magnesium, and also a source of choline, l-tyrosine and antioxidants.

SERVES 4 CHILDREN ⓥⓓⓟⓒⓞⓛ

200 g/7 oz cooked brown basmati rice
100 g/3¹/₂ oz spring greens or leeks, finely chopped
1 small red pepper, deseeded and finely chopped
100 g/3¹/₂ oz frozen sweetcorn kernels, cooked
2 tbsp grated Cheddar or Parmesan cheese
2 small eggs, beaten
2 tbsp plain flour
pinch of salt
2 tbsp light olive oil
pepper

1 Mix all the ingredients, except the oil, together in a bowl, with pepper to taste, to make a loose batter.

2 Heat half the oil in a large, non-stick frying pan over a medium-high heat. When hot, drop 1 large spoonful of the batter (about one-eighth) into the frying pan, followed by a further 3 large spoonfuls. Cook for 2–3 minutes until golden on the underside, then flip over and cook the other side. Remove to a warmed plate covered with kitchen paper, with a slotted spoon.

3 Heat the remaining oil in the frying pan and repeat with the remaining batter.

4 Serve the fritters warm.

Cook's Tips
* This is a good way of getting children to eat some vegetables.

Variations
* You can vary the vegetables used to suit what you have to hand. For example, you could add finely sliced mushrooms, courgettes, aubergine and spring onions.
* Add some spices, such as 1 teaspoon of paprika or ground cumin, or 1 tablespoon of chopped fresh herbs, such as parsley.

Veggie Burgers

NUTRITION NOTES These burgers are a good source of vitamins B6 and E, folate and carotene, and also a source of choline, selenium, iron and antioxidants.

SERVES 4 CHILDREN ⓋⒹⓅⒸⓄⓁ
1 onion, roughly chopped
1 celery stick, roughly chopped
1 carrot, roughly chopped
400 g/14 oz canned mixed beans, drained and rinsed
1 garlic clove, chopped
1 tbsp chopped fresh parsley
1 tbsp tomato purée
1 tbsp light soy sauce
40 g/1½ oz fresh wholemeal breadcrumbs
1 egg, beaten
1 tbsp groundnut or light olive oil

1 Put the onion, celery and carrot in a blender or food processor and process for 20–30 seconds until all the vegetables are very finely chopped.

2 Put the beans in a large bowl and mash thoroughly with a fork. Add the vegetables, garlic, parsley, tomato purée and soy sauce and mix together thoroughly. Add the breadcrumbs and egg and mix well.

3 Form the mixture into 8 small burgers or 4 large ones.

4 Heat the oil in a large, non-stick frying pan over a medium-high heat, add the burgers and cook for 5 minutes, or until the undersides are golden. Turn over and cook for a further 3–4 minutes. Serve immediately.

Cook's Tip
* Serve the burgers in burger buns or with a small portion of oven chips, with a leafy salad on the side.

Variations
* You can use all canned chickpeas or lentils, or any combination of canned pulses for this recipe.
* Add some chopped fresh deseeded chilli for a spicier burger.

Cheesy Pasta Bake

NUTRITION NOTES This pasta bake is an excellent source of vitamins C, E, B2 and B12, carotene and magnesium.

SERVES 4 CHILDREN ⓋⓅⒸⓁ
2 tbsp olive oil
2 yellow peppers, deseeded and chopped
1 mild onion, finely chopped
1 small aubergine, chopped
400 g/14 oz canned chopped tomatoes with herbs
1 tbsp tomato purée
2 tbsp hot water, plus extra if needed
pinch of salt
250 g/9 oz dried wholewheat pasta spirals
100 g/3½ oz Cheddar cheese, grated
40 g/1½ oz slightly stale wholemeal or white breadcrumbs
pepper

1 Heat the oil in a large, non-stick frying pan over a medium heat, add the yellow peppers, onion and aubergine and cook, stirring occasionally, for 15 minutes, or until soft.

2 Add the tomatoes and their juice, tomato purée, hot water, salt and pepper to taste to the frying pan and stir well. Bring to a simmer and cook for 15 minutes. Stir in a little more water if the mixture is not fairly sloppy. Preheat the oven to 190°C/375°F/Gas Mark 5.

3 Meanwhile, cook the pasta in a large saucepan of lightly salted boiling water for 15 minutes, or according to the packet instructions, until al dente. Drain and tip into a suitably sized, shallow ovenproof dish. Add the tomato mixture and mix together well. Spread out evenly in the dish.

4 Mix the Cheddar cheese and breadcrumbs together, then sprinkle evenly over the pasta mixture. Bake in the preheated oven for 20–25 minutes until the top is golden. Serve immediately.

Variation
* You can add pieces of cooked tuna or chicken to the bake at the end of Step 3, if you like.

Thin-crust Vegetable Pizza

NUTRITION NOTES This pizza is an excellent source of carotene, vitamins B6, B12 and E, selenium and magnesium, and is also a good source of vitamin C and choline.

SERVES 4 CHILDREN ⓥ ⒟ ⒫ ⒸⓁ

2 tbsp olive oil

1 sweet potato, peeled and cut into small cubes

1 Spanish onion, finely chopped

250 ml/9 fl oz canned chopped tomatoes

1 tbsp sun-dried tomato paste

2 tsp chopped fresh oregano or 1 tsp dried oregano

1 large tomato, thinly sliced

100 g/3½ oz mozzarella or mature Cheddar cheese, grated

PIZZA BASE

125 g/4½ oz wholemeal flour

125 g/4½ oz strong white flour, plus extra for dusting

pinch of salt

½ tsp easy-blend dried yeast

150 ml/5 fl oz warm water

1 tbsp olive oil, plus extra for brushing and drizzling

1 To make the pizza base, sift the flours and salt together into a bowl and stir in the yeast. Make a well in the centre and pour in the water and oil. Mix with a fork to form a soft dough, then knead on a floured surface for 10 minutes, or until smooth. Cover with a damp, clean cloth and set aside in a warm place for 1 hour, or until the dough has doubled in size.

2 Meanwhile, heat half the oil in a non-stick frying pan over a medium-high heat, add the sweet potato cubes and cook, stirring occasionally, for 5 minutes, or until soft and golden. Remove with a slotted spoon and set aside. Add the onion and cook, stirring occasionally, for 10 minutes. Add the canned tomatoes and their juice, sun-dried tomato paste and oregano, stir and simmer for a further 15 minutes. Leave to cool.

3 Preheat the oven to 200°C/400°F/Gas Mark 6. Lightly brush a 30-cm/12-inch pizza tin with oil. When the dough is ready, turn it out onto a floured work surface, knock it back and roll out thinly into a 35-cm/14-inch round.

4 Arrange the dough in the prepared pizza tin, lightly brush with oil and spread the tomato sauce over the top, followed by the sweet potato, the fresh tomato slices and the mozzarella cheese. Drizzle over a little oil and bake in the preheated oven for 25–30 minutes, or until the top is bubbling and the base is golden at the edges. Serve immediately.

Cook's Tip
* You can save time by using ready-prepared pizza dough or a ready-made pizza dough mix – follow the packet instructions.

Butternut and Bean Casserole

SERVES 4–6 CHILDREN ⒟Ⓟ©Ⓛ

2 tbsp olive oil

4 skinless, boneless chicken thighs, about 100 g/3$^1/_2$ oz each,
   cut into bite-sized pieces

1 large onion, sliced

2 leeks, chopped

2 garlic cloves, chopped

1 butternut squash, peeled, deseeded and cut into cubes

2 carrots, diced

400 g/14 oz canned chopped tomatoes and herbs

400 g/14 oz canned mixed beans, drained and rinsed

100 ml/3$^1/_2$ fl oz vegetable or chicken stock, plus extra if needed

salt and pepper

NUTRITION NOTES This casserole is an excellent source of choline, vitamins B6, C and E, folate, selenium, zinc and carotene, and also a source of iron and antioxidants.

1 Preheat the oven to 160°C/325°F/Gas Mark 3.

2 Heat half the oil in a large, flameproof casserole over a high heat, add the chicken and cook, turning frequently, for 2–3 minutes until browned all over. Reduce the heat to medium, remove the chicken with a slotted spoon and set aside.

3 Add the remaining oil to the casserole, add the onion and leeks and cook, stirring occasionally, for 10 minutes, or until soft. Add the garlic, squash and carrots and cook, stirring, for 2 minutes. Add the tomatoes and their juice, beans and stock, stir well and bring to a simmer.

4 Cover, transfer to the preheated oven and cook for 1–1$^1/_4$ hours, stirring once or twice – if the casserole looks too dry, add a little extra stock. Season with a very little salt and pepper to taste before serving.

Cook's Tips
* You can serve the casserole with green vegetables, such as cabbage, spinach or broccoli.
* For vegetarians, you can omit the chicken.

Three-colour Italian Omelette (Frittata)

NUTRITION NOTES This omelette is an excellent source of choline, vitamins B6, B12 and C, folate and carotene.

SERVES 4 CHILDREN Ⓥ Ⓓ Ⓟ Ⓒ Ⓞ Ⓛ

2 tbsp olive oil

2 red peppers, deseeded and thinly sliced

2 courgettes, thinly sliced

75 g/2³/₄ oz broccoli, cut into mini florets, or frozen petits pois, cooked

4 spring onions, chopped

2 large tomatoes, deseeded and chopped

8 large eggs

3 tbsp freshly grated Parmesan cheese

1 tbsp cold water

salt and pepper

1 handful fresh basil leaves, chopped, to garnish

1 Heat the oil in a large, non-stick frying pan over a high heat, add the red peppers, courgettes and broccoli and cook, stirring, for 3 minutes, or until just softened. Add the spring onions and tomatoes and cook, stirring, for 1 minute. Reduce the heat to medium-low. (If using petits pois instead of broccoli, stir in now.)

2 Put the eggs, Parmesan cheese and water in a bowl with a little salt and pepper to taste and beat together. Pour the egg mixture evenly over the vegetables in the frying pan. Cook, without stirring, for 6–8 minutes, or until the underside of the omelette is cooked and golden but the top is still runny. Meanwhile, preheat the grill to high.

3 Put the frying pan under the preheated grill and cook the omelette for 2 minutes, or until the top is cooked and golden, and it is set all the way through. Cut the omelette into 4 wedges, and scatter with the basil to garnish.

Cook's Tip

* Serve with a mixed-leaf side salad and some crusty bread.

Meatballs with Tomato Sauce

NUTRITION NOTES This dish is an excellent source of l-tyrosine, vitamins B6 and B12, carotene, zinc and iron, and also a good source of vitamins C and E and antioxidants.

SERVES 4 CHILDREN ⒹⓅ©ⓆⓁ

3 tbsp olive oil

3 onions, finely chopped

3 garlic cloves, crushed

2 heaped tsp dried mixed herbs or oregano

450 g/1 lb fresh beef mince

1 large egg, beaten

salt and pepper

2–3 tbsp freshly grated Parmesan or mozzarella cheese, to serve

TOMATO SAUCE

400 g/14 oz canned chopped tomatoes

1 tbsp tomato purée

pinch of soft light brown sugar

1 Heat 2 tablespoons of the oil in a saucepan over a medium heat, add the onions and cook, stirring occasionally, for 5 minutes, or until transparent. Add the garlic and cook, stirring, for a further minute, then stir in the herbs. Transfer half the contents of the saucepan to a bowl and leave to cool slightly.

2 To make the tomato sauce, add all the sauce ingredients, with a very little salt and pepper to taste, to the saucepan, stir well and bring to a simmer. Simmer for 20–30 minutes, stirring once or twice, until you have a rich sauce. Meanwhile, stir the mince, egg and a very little salt and pepper to taste into the onion mixture in the bowl. Combine thoroughly and then form into 16 small balls.

3 When the tomato sauce is nearly ready, heat the remaining oil in a non-stick frying pan over a medium-high heat, add the meatballs and cook, turning a few times, for 5–6 minutes, or until golden on all sides and cooked through. Serve with the tomato sauce, with the cheese sprinkled over.

Cook's Tip

* Serve on a bowl of steaming wholewheat spaghetti or other pasta shapes, or alternatively serve with mashed potatoes or rice.

Beef Chow Mein with Beansprouts

NUTRITION NOTES This dish is an excellent source of l-tyrosine, vitamins B6 and B12, carotene, zinc and iron, and also a source of vitamins C and E, magnesium and antioxidants.

SERVES 4 CHILDREN ⒹⓅ©ⓆⓁ

250 g/9 oz dried medium thread egg noodles

2 tbsp light soy sauce

2 tsp caster sugar

100 ml/3$\frac{1}{2}$ fl oz beef stock

1 tsp cornflour or sauce flour

2 tbsp groundnut oil

350 g/12 oz minute or rump steak, cut into thin strips

1 garlic clove, finely chopped

1 onion, thinly sliced

2 carrots, thinly sliced

200 g/7 oz fresh beansprouts

1 tbsp sesame oil

1 Cook the noodles in a large saucepan of boiling water for 3–4 minutes, or according to the packet instructions, until just tender. Drain and keep warm.

2 Mix the soy sauce, sugar, stock and cornflour together in a small bowl.

3 Heat the groundnut oil in a preheated wok or large, non-stick frying pan over a high heat, add the steak and stir-fry for 2 minutes. Add the garlic, onion and carrots, and stir-fry for 2–3 minutes.

4 Add the soy sauce mixture and cook, stirring, for 1 minute until the sauce thickens a little, then add the beansprouts and stir again. Toss the mixture with the noodles and sesame oil in the wok or frying pan and serve immediately.

Variation

* You can use chicken or pork instead of the beef steak.

Breakfasts, Bakes and Desserts

There is no need to deny yourself or your family some sweet treats – desserts, breakfasts and bakes can be a good opportunity to get healthy foods such as fresh and dried fruits, nuts and seeds into everyone's diet. All the recipes in this chapter are easy to make and don't take too long, and are packed with nutrients to help boost your brainpower.

KEY
Ⓥ Suitable for vegetarians
Ⓓ Ideal for weight control
Ⓟ Suitable for pregnancy
Ⓒ Suitable for children
Ⓠ Quick to prepare and cook
Ⓛ Low cost

Yogurt and Strawberry Smoothie

NUTRITION NOTES This smoothie is a good source of vitamins B12 and C, and also a source of antioxidants and l-tyrosine.

SERVES 2 Ⓥ Ⓓ Ⓟ Ⓒ Ⓠ Ⓛ

6 ice cubes
1 small banana, peeled and roughly chopped
200 g/7 oz fresh strawberries, hulled and roughly chopped
150 ml/5 fl oz natural bio yogurt
150 ml/5 fl oz semi-skimmed milk
1 tbsp runny honey

1 Put the ice cubes in a blender and process until crushed. Add all the remaining ingredients and blend until smooth.

2 Pour into 2 tall glasses and serve immediately.

Cook's Tip
* This can be served as either a breakfast or a dessert in a glass.

Variation
* You can vary the fresh fruit according to what is available or to taste – for example, try raspberries instead of strawberries.

Oat and Nut Crunch Mix

NUTRITION NOTES This mix is an excellent source of vitamins B1, B6 and E, folate, iron, magnesium, zinc, selenium and antioxidants, and also a source of l-tyrosine, carotene and omega-3 fatty acids.

SERVES 8 Ⓥ Ⓓ Ⓟ Ⓒ (aged over 5 years), Ⓠ Ⓛ

groundnut oil, for brushing
90 g/3¹/₄ oz jumbo oats
25 g/1 oz pine kernels
40 g/1¹/₂ oz pistachio nuts or hazelnuts
40 g/1¹/₂ oz almonds
40 g/1¹/₂ oz Brazil nuts, roughly chopped
2 tbsp sunflower seeds
2 tbsp pumpkin seeds
1 tbsp flax seeds
50 g/1³/₄ oz dried ready-to-eat apricots, chopped
40 g/1¹/₂ oz sultanas
1 tsp ground cinnamon

1 Heat a non-stick frying pan over a medium heat and brush with a little oil. Add the oats and pine kernels and cook, stirring constantly, for 8–10 minutes, or until they smell nutty and look a little golden. Leave to cool.

2 Transfer the toasted oat mixture to a large bowl, add all the remaining ingredients and mix together well. Store in a lidded, airtight container in the refrigerator.

Cook's Tips
* The mix will keep for up to 2 weeks in the refrigerator.
* It makes a nice topping for yogurt or fruit, can be stirred into breakfast cereals to make them more nutritious and is ideal as a between-meal snack.

Fruit Crudités with Chocolate Sauce

NUTRITION NOTES This dish is an excellent source of vitamin C and a good source of iron and antioxidants.

SERVES 4 ⓥⒹⓅⒸⓆⓁ
200 g/7 oz good-quality plain chocolate, at least 60% cocoa solids
12 fresh strawberries
2 fresh pineapple rings
1 orange
1 large banana
4 tbsp semi-skimmed milk, at room temperature

1 Break the chocolate into a heatproof bowl that will fit snugly over a small saucepan on the hob so that when you put 2 cm/ ³/₄ inch water in the saucepan, the base of the bowl doesn't touch the water. Set the bowl over the saucepan and heat the water to a slow simmer. Leave the chocolate, undisturbed, to melt very slowly – this will take about 10 minutes.

2 Meanwhile, prepare the fruit. Hull the strawberries and, if large, halve. Remove the central core from the pineapple rings and cut the flesh into chunks. Peel the orange, and remove all the pith. Cut the flesh into segments. Peel the banana and cut into 4-cm/1¹/₂-inch chunks. Arrange the fruit on a platter.

3 When the chocolate has melted, remove the bowl from the saucepan and stir in the milk. Pour the sauce into a serving bowl and serve with the fruit for dipping.

Variations
* You can use a variety of fruits – try mango, nectarine and satsuma for a change.
* Alternatively, you can pour the sauce into individual dishes and divide the fruit into 4 portions to serve.

Fresh Fruit Salad with Blueberries

NUTRITION NOTES This fruit salad is an excellent source of vitamin C and antioxidants.

SERVES 4 ⓥⒹⓅⒸⓆⓁ
2 red-skinned eating apples
1 dessert pear
1 tbsp freshly squeezed lemon juice
100 g/3¹/₂ oz red seedless grapes
2 kiwi fruit
100 g/3¹/₂ oz fresh blueberries
150 ml/5 fl oz apple juice

1 Core and slice the apples. Peel, core and slice the pear. Put the apple and pear slices in a non-metallic serving bowl, sprinkle over the lemon juice and toss well.

2 Halve the grapes and add to the bowl. Peel, halve and slice the kiwi fruit, then add to the bowl with the remaining ingredients. Stir, then cover and chill in the refrigerator for 2–3 hours. Stir once or twice before serving.

Cook's Tip
* Serve with one or two spoonfuls of natural fromage frais or bio yogurt, or serve as a breakfast with the Oat and Nut Crunch Mix and yogurt.

Walnut and Banana Cake

MAKES ABOUT 12 SLICES Ⓥ Ⓟ Ⓒ (aged over 5 years), Ⓝ Ⓛ

250 g/9 oz wholemeal plain flour

1 tsp salt

1 heaped tsp baking powder

1 tsp ground cinnamon

4 ripe bananas

100 ml/3¹/₂ fl oz groundnut oil, plus extra for oiling

25 g/1 oz unsalted butter, at room temperature

175 g/6 oz soft light brown sugar

2 large eggs, beaten

175 g/6 oz walnut pieces

> **NUTRITION NOTES** This cake is a good source of vitamins B1 and B6, magnesium and selenium, and also a source of omega-3 fatty acids, choline, folate and vitamin E.

1 Preheat the oven to 180°C/350°F/Gas Mark 4. Lightly oil a 1-kg/ 2 lb 4-oz cake or loaf tin.

2 Sift the flour, salt, baking powder and cinnamon together into a large bowl, then add the larger particles left in the sieve. Stir thoroughly with a fork.

3 Peel the bananas and mash with a fork. Add to the bowl with all the remaining ingredients, except the nuts. Using an electric hand-held whisk, beat the mixture until smooth. Alternatively, use a wooden spoon. Fold in the walnuts.

4 Spoon the mixture into the prepared tin and level the surface. Bake in the preheated oven for 1–1 ¹/₄ hours, or until a skewer inserted into the centre comes out clean. Leave to cool in the tin for a few minutes, then turn out onto a wire rack to cool completely before serving. Alternatively, the cake can be stored in an airtight tin for up to 5 days.

Cook's Tips

* Make sure that the butter is soft when you add it to the mixture.
* If the mixture isn't a good 'dropping' consistency after beating, beat in 1–2 tablespoons water.

Carrot Cake

MAKES ABOUT 12 SLICES Ⓥ Ⓟ Ⓒ Ⓛ

3 large eggs
200 g/7 oz soft light brown sugar
175 ml/6 fl oz groundnut oil, plus extra for oiling
100 g/3^1/$_2$ oz white plain flour
100 g/3^1/$_2$ oz wholemeal plain flour
2 tsp baking powder
1 heaped tsp ground cinnamon
1 tsp salt
1 tsp vanilla extract
3 carrots, grated
juice of 1 orange
100 g/3^1/$_2$ oz sultanas

1 Preheat the oven to 180°C/350°F/Gas Mark 4. Lightly oil a 1-kg/2 lb 4-oz cake or loaf tin.

2 Beat the eggs in a large bowl, then add the sugar and beat again. Add the oil and beat until well combined, then add all the remaining ingredients and stir until thoroughly mixed.

3 Tip the mixture into the prepared tin and level the surface. Bake in the preheated oven for 1 hour, or until a skewer inserted into the centre comes out clean. Leave to cool in the tin for a few minutes, then turn out onto a wire rack and leave to cool before serving.

Variations
* You can make a simple icing by mixing together 200 g/7 oz 8 per cent-fat natural fromage frais, 2 tablespoons of icing sugar and the juice of half a lemon.
* You can use raisins or chopped, dried ready-to-eat apricots instead of the sultanas, or omit the fruit altogether. You can also use chopped nuts – for those over 5 years only.

Blueberry and Banana Muffins

NUTRITION NOTES These muffins are a good source of vitamins B1, B6 and B12, magnesium and selenium, and a source of vitamins E and C, folate and antioxidants.

MAKES 12 ⓋⒹⓅⒸⓆⓁ
100 g/3¹/₂ oz wholemeal plain flour
150 g/5¹/₂ oz white self-raising flour
1 tsp baking powder
1 tsp ground cinnamon
100 g/3¹/₂ oz soft light brown caster sugar
250 ml/9 fl oz buttermilk or semi-skimmed milk
1 large egg, beaten
100 ml/3¹/₂ fl oz groundnut oil
1 large ripe banana, peeled and well mashed
200 g/7 oz fresh blueberries

1 Preheat the oven to 200°C/400°F/Gas Mark 6. Line a 12-hole muffin tin with paper muffin cases.

2 Sift the flours, baking powder and cinnamon together into a large bowl, then stir in the sugar.

3 In a separate bowl, mix the buttermilk, egg, oil and banana together. Add to the dry ingredients and stir until just combined – do not overmix. Stir in the blueberries.

4 Spoon the mixture into the paper cases. Bake in the preheated oven for 20–25 minutes until risen and golden. Leave to cool in the tin for a few minutes, then transfer to a wire rack to cool completely. Store in an airtight container – they will keep for 1–2 days.

Cook's Tips
* Make sure that the banana is well mashed until almost liquid.
* Buttermilk is available in supermarkets and health-food stores.

Variation
* You can use other fresh fruit, such as raspberries or blackberries, instead of the blueberries.

Oaty Apple and Cinnamon Muffins

NUTRITION NOTES These muffins are a source of choline, vitamins B1, B6, B12 and E, folate, magnesium and selenium.

MAKES 12 ⓋⓅⒸⓆⓁ
200 g/7 oz wholemeal plain flour
75 g/2³/₄ oz fine oatmeal
2 tsp baking powder
125 g/4¹/₂ oz soft light brown sugar
2 large eggs
225 ml/8 fl oz semi-skimmed milk
100 ml/3¹/₂ fl oz groundnut oil
1 tsp vanilla extract
1 tsp ground cinnamon
1 large cooking apple

1 Preheat the oven to 180°C/350°F/Gas Mark 4. Line a 12-hole muffin tin with paper muffin cases.

2 Sift the flour, oatmeal and baking powder together into a large bowl, then add the larger particles left in the sieve. Stir in the sugar. In a separate bowl, beat the eggs, milk and oil together until well combined. Add to the dry ingredients, along with the vanilla extract and cinnamon, and stir until just combined – do not overmix.

3 Peel, core and grate the apple, then stir into the mixture. Spoon the mixture into the paper cases and bake in the preheated oven for 20–25 minutes until risen and golden brown. Leave to cool in the tin for a few minutes before serving warm, or transfer to a wire rack to cool completely.

Variation
* You can use 150 ml/5 fl oz stewed or puréed apple instead of the raw apple.

Chocolate Nut Brownies

NUTRITION NOTES These brownies are a source of choline, iron, omega-3 fatty acids, vitamins B1, B12 and E, folate and magnesium.

MAKES 16 SQUARES Ⓥ Ⓟ Ⓒ (aged over 5 years), Ⓠ Ⓛ
groundnut oil, for oiling
225 g/8 oz good-quality plain chocolate, at least 60% cocoa solids
175 g/6 oz low-cholesterol spread
3 large eggs
100 g/3½ oz caster sugar
175 g/6 oz self-raising flour
100 g/3½ oz walnuts or blanched hazelnuts, chopped
50 g/1¾ oz milk chocolate chips

1 Preheat the oven to 180°C/350°F/Gas Mark 4. Lightly oil a non-stick, shallow baking tin about 25 cm/10 inches square.

2 Break the chocolate into a heatproof bowl that will fit snugly over a small saucepan on the hob so that when you put 2 cm/¾ inch water in the saucepan, the base of the bowl doesn't touch the water.

3 Add the spread to the chocolate, set the bowl over the saucepan and heat the water to a slow simmer. Leave the chocolate, undisturbed, to melt very slowly – this will take about 10 minutes. Remove the bowl from the saucepan and stir well to combine the chocolate and spread.

4 Meanwhile, beat the eggs and sugar together in a bowl until pale cream coloured. Stir in the melted chocolate mixture and then the flour, nuts and chocolate chips. Mix everything together well.

5 Tip the mixture into the prepared baking tin and bake in the preheated oven for 30 minutes, or until the top is set – if the centre is still slightly sticky, that will be all the better. Leave to cool in the tin, then lift out and cut into squares.

Cook's Tip
* Serve with some Greek-style yogurt for an indulgent dessert.

Walnut and Seed Bread

NUTRITION NOTES This bread is a good source of vitamins B1 and B6, magnesium and selenium, and also a source of omega-3 fatty acids, folate, vitamin E, iron and zinc.

MAKES ABOUT 12 SLICES Ⓥ Ⓓ Ⓟ Ⓒ (aged over 5 years), Ⓛ
450 g/1 lb wholemeal or multigrain bread flour, plus extra for dusting
75 g/2¾ oz oat flour
1 tsp salt
1 tsp soft dark brown sugar
2 tsp easy-blend dried yeast
125 g/4½ oz walnuts, chopped
25 g/1 oz pumpkin seeds
300 ml/10 fl oz warm water, plus extra if needed
1 tbsp olive or walnut oil, plus extra for oiling

1 Lightly oil a 2 lb 4-oz/1kg loaf tin.

2 Tip the flours into a large bowl and sprinkle over the salt, sugar and yeast, then the walnuts and pumpkin seeds. Combine thoroughly with a fork. Make a well in the centre and pour in the water and oil. Mix to form a dough, adding a little more water as necessary.

3 When the dough has come together and the bowl is clean, turn the dough out onto a lightly floured surface and knead for 10 minutes until smooth. Shape to fit the prepared loaf tin. Cover with a clean, damp cloth and leave to rise in a warm place for about 1 hour, or until almost doubled in size.

4 Meanwhile, preheat the oven to 220°C/425°F/Gas Mark 7. Uncover the dough and bake in the preheated oven for 30 minutes, or until the base of the loaf sounds hollow when tapped with your knuckles. Turn the loaf out and leave to cool on a wire rack.

Variation
* You can vary the seeds and nuts that you add, but walnuts and pumpkin seeds are particularly good sources of omega-3 fatty acids compared with most other nuts and seeds.

Index

B

bananas
  blueberry and banana muffins
    92
  walnut and banana cake 90
beans
  baked sea bass with white bean
    purée 44
  butternut and bean casserole 80
  chunky sweet potato and butter
    bean soup 24
  easy bean dip with crudités 30
  ribollito (Tuscan bean soup) 21
  veggie burgers 76
beef
  beef chow mein with bean
    sprouts 83
  beef satay with peanut sauce 66
  chilli beef with avocado
    salsa 64
  hoisin beef with mushrooms 66
  meatballs with tomato
    sauce 83
blueberries
  blueberry and banana muffins
    92
  fresh fruit salad with blueberries
    89
  butternut and bean casserole 80

C

carrot cake 91
casseroles
  butternut and bean casserole 80
  Turkish lamb casserole 62
  warmly spiced vegetable
    casserole 54
chicken
  butternut and bean casserole 80
  spicy chicken with tortilla wrap
    61
  sweet chilli chicken with Creole
    rice 59
chickpeas
  couscous, nut and chickpea
    pilaf 28
  red pepper felafel with
    hummus dressing 58
chilli beef with avocado salsa 64

chocolate
  chocolate nut brownies 95
  fruit crudités with chocolate
    sauce 89
couscous, nut and chickpea pilaf
    28

E

eggs
  eggs and peppers on toast 33
  ratatouille with poached
    eggs 54
  three-colour Italian omelette
    (frittata) 81
  traditional Spanish omelette
    with herb salad 56

F

fish
  angler's filo pie 42
  baked sea bass with white bean
    purée 44
  Chinese herring fillets 47
  creamy salmon baked potatoes
    30
  creamy salmon pasta 71
  grilled salmon with green lentils
    and caper sauce 40
  Italian fish soup with white
    wine 25
  quick smoked mackerel pâté 33
  real fish nuggets 71
  red mullet parcels with olives 44
  rice, salmon and pesto salad 28
  salmon fish cakes 75
  salmon potato patties with
    jalapeño 43
  spiced mackerel with tomato
    salad 39
  swordfish steaks with lemon
    dressing 37
  Thai swordfish kebabs 37
  tuna, lentil and potato
    salad 27
  tuna pasta bake 72
  tuna steaks with Catalan sauce
    39
fritters
  vegetable fritters 75

H

hoisin beef with mushrooms 66

L

lamb
  lamb kebabs with Greek salad 62
  tray-baked lamb steaks with
    tomatoes 61
  Turkish lamb casserole 62
lentils
  grilled salmon with green lentils
    and caper sauce 40
  tomato, lentil and red pepper
    soup 21
  tuna, lentil and potato salad 27

N

nuts
  beef satay with peanut sauce 66
  chocolate nut brownies 95
  couscous, nut and chickpea
    pilaf 28
  oat and nut crunch mix 86
  teriyaki prawns with cashew
    nuts 51
  walnut and banana cake 90
  walnut and seed bread 95

O

oats
  oat and nut crunch mix 86
  oaty apple and cinnamon
    muffins 92

P

pasta
  cheesy pasta bake 76
  creamy salmon pasta 71
  tuna pasta bake 72
peppers
  eggs and peppers on toast 33
  red pepper felafel with hummus
    dressing 58
  tomato, lentil and red pepper
    soup 21
pizza, thin-crust vegetable 79
potatoes
  creamy salmon baked
    potatoes 30

salmon potato patties with
    jalapeño 43
tuna, lentil and potato salad 27

R

rice
  rice, salmon and pesto salad 28
  sweet chilli chicken with Creole
    rice 59
  seafood paella with saffron
    rice 48

S

salads
  gado gado (Indonesian warm
    salad) 22
  lamb kebabs with Greek
    salad 62
  rice, salmon and pesto salad 28
  spiced mackerel with tomato
    salad 39
  traditional Spanish omelette
    with herb salad 56
seafood
  chilli crab cakes with stir-fried
    greens 50
  paella with saffron rice 48
  seafood provençale 47
  teriyaki prawns with cashew
    nuts 51
strawberries
  yogurt and strawberry smoothie
    86
sweet potatoes
  chunky sweet potato and butter
    bean soup 24

T

tomatoes
  meatballs with tomato sauce 83
  spiced mackerel with tomato
    salad 39
  tomato, lentil and red pepper
    soup 21
  tray-baked lamb steaks with
    tomatoes 61

Y

yogurt and strawberry smoothie 86